ICELAND FROM ABOVE
land in creation

ICELAND FROM ABOVE
land in creation

TEXT AND PHOTOGRAPHS BY BJÖRN RÚRIKSSON

⊙ GEOSCAN-JARÐSYN SELFOSS

CONTENTS

Introduction	6	The North	90
Central volcanoes	8	Lake Mývatn	98
The South	34	The East	106
The Southern Highlands	56	The Interior Highlands	116
The West	72	Technical information	128
The Western Fjords	80		

ISBN 978-9979-56-022-7 (English edition)
Third edition February 2018; © Text and Photographs, Design/Layout: Björn Rúriksson.
Typography: Optima 9.5 pt. Printed in the Czech Republic.
Published by: Jardsýn, Jadar 5, 800 Selfoss, Iceland. Email: bjornrur@gmail.com Tel: +354-777 6130.
Photos on front cover, pages 15 and 16, and on the back flyleaf by Siripan Raksa,
Photo on page 22 by Birkir Örn Björnsson. Photo on page 61 (lower) by Rúrik Karl Björnsson.
Translation: Dr. Georg Douglas. The book will also be available at IcelandFromAbove.net

Photo right: Viewed eastwards on 5th of September 2014 at 10:10 GMT.
The 2000 m high bowl-like *Bárðarbunga* volcano is smothered by 800 metres of ice
below the flat area in the upper right of the photograph. Measurements indicate that
magma is migrating from the volcano centre into the dyke swarm to the northeast.
Magma surfaced at 40 km distance from *Bárðarbunga* in *Holuhraun* where the eruption
is currently taking place (steam column in the background). *Herðubreið* on horizon left.

Page 3: *Múlajökull* stretches out on the land below *Hofsjökull* like a bear's paw.

Front cover: Lake Lödmundarvatn in the southern highlands.

Back cover: Fierce volcanic activity along a new fissure in *Holuhraun*
viewed directly from above on 5th of September 2014 at 09:35 GMT.

INTRODUCTION

At the time of first printing in 2014, the *Bárðarbunga* volcanic system had erupted and been active for a little over a week, evoking memories of the 2010 *Eyjafjallajökull* eruption which caused worldwide chaos for six days.

The large subglacial *Bárðarbunga* volcano sits on top of the active hot mantle plume under Iceland with the biggest eruptions happening in prehistoric times. The new eruption is opening up along an underground dyke intrusion, where magma drains from *Bárðarbunga* and surfaces some 40 km northeast of the volcano itself.

Volcanism from more than 30 active volcanoes, glaciers and the sea play the main part in shaping the landscape.

Volcanic activity has been vigorous in the past few years and decades. For centuries *Hekla* has erupted at intervals ranging from 5 to 6 decades and every ten years since 1970. *Krafla* in the North was active from 1975 until 1984, with lava flowing on numerous occasions. The eruption in *Eyjafjallajökull* in 2010 aroused worldwide interest, as did the *Heimaey* eruption which had major disruptive effects in settled areas in 1973. The present and recent volcanic activity in *Vatnajökull*, sometimes with associated jökulhlaups (catastrophic floods) like in 1996 shows us clearly the danger and destruction inherent in subglacial volcanism.

Iceland differs greatly from most of its neighbouring countries. When seen from the air it more closely resembles the primeval earth and is in effect a huge natural history museum of great variety under an open sky. This book is intended to give an insight to the vast and beautiful world of Icelandic nature and all the fascinating processes which build up the land - and tear it down!

Björn Rúriksson

Spectacularly thin lavaflow from the southernmost craters at *Holuhraun*.

CENTRAL VOLCANOES

Beneath a central volcano, there is a magma chamber in which magma constantly accumulates from below. Diverging plate movement weakens the crust, and faults and fissure swarms develop. Molten magma penetrates into these fissures, sometimes far from the volcano itself. *Hekla, Katla, Eyjafjallajökull, Grímsvötn* and *Bárðarbunga* all bear characteristics of a central volcano.

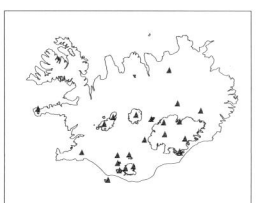

Most volcanic eruptions in Iceland are associated with central volcanoes. During the past century eruptions have occurred on average at intervals of every 3-4 years. Almost none of the 250 eruptions which have occurred since the Settlement of Iceland are large on a world scale, with the exception of a very few which have caused great damage, including the *Laki* eruption of 1783 which was one of the largest eruptions on Earth in historical time and caused widespread crop failure in the northern hemisphere. The well publicised *Eyjafjallajökull* eruption which began on 14th April 2010 caused little damage in Iceland itself, but much more abroad. Aviation in Europe practically ceased completely for almost a week, as well as connecting flights in many other parts of the world. Most of the recent eruptions have occurred in volcanoes in the southern half of the country, with the newest activity taking place at *Bárðarbunga in September 2014*. Apart from the eruptions in and around *Eyjafjallajökull* in 2010, *Hekla* has been very active. Some eruptions have occurred in *Vatnajökull*, where an eruption and associated flood (*icel. jökulhlaup*) in November 1996 caused great damage to roads and bridges.

A view of *Gígjökull* before the eruption. This was the channel of the floodwater.

Spectacular activity in the *Norðri* crater as molten rock spawns lava streams in all directions.

Lava fountains in the *Suðri* crater. A river of molten lava flows to the NW.

The vast wilderness north of *Vatnajökull* provides the dramatic stage for the *Holuhraun* eruption. *Askja* and *Herðubreið* in the background.

Looking north on 5th of September from *Dyngjujökull* across *Holuhraun* (from 1797) towards the erupting craters. The Central volcano *Askja* in the background.

Looking southwards across lava fountains
in *Baugur* on 5th of September 2014. *Dyngjujökull*
in the background is partly obscured by gas emissions from the eruption.

The 100 m heigh lava fountains from the
Baugur crater. Rapidly flowing lava from the crater can be seen in background.

The boiling inferno bubbling on the lava surface where fissures opened up in *Holuhraun* during the early hours of 5th of September 2014. Magma melting its way through the old sandy lava from 1797. An incipient fissure and possible craters can be seen forming.

A new fissure and craters having just opened up in the thin and weak hot crust.

The lava fountains from the three craters; *Norðri, Baugur* and *Suðri*.

Similar crater eruptions occurred in the
Krafla area in North Iceland in the years 1975-1984.
A new crater is born during the last eruption in September of 1984.

Pages 18/19: Looking across *Suðri's* lavaflow to the crater *Baugur*.

The *Fimmvörðuháls* craters of the *Eyjafjallajökull* volcano, on 4th April 2010. Lava works of art illuminate the surroundings (photo left) or create steam clouds in contact with snow (photo right).

Overleaf: the summit crater produced hair-fine ash which traveled in the upper atmosphere to Europe, disrupting aviation for many days.

Powerful ash and steam columns on the first day of the *Hekla* eruption, 17th of August 1980. Judging from photos taken from a distance of 100 km the column rose to between 20-25 kilometres. Lava fountains were active from the summit crater and down the ridge axis all along the southwestern fissure. The picture on the left is taken above the cloud layer and that on the right from below.

The floodwater channel underneath the ice on its course from *Grímsvötn* down its 50 km journey to the glacier's snout in November 1996. The roof above the floodwater collapsed when the flood level fell. This channel southeast of the *Grímsvötn* caldera is 6 km long, 1 km wide and 100 m deep.

The eruption started between *Bárðarbunga* and *Grímsvötn* on 30th of September 1996. The eruption emerged through 500-700 m thick ice north of the *Grímsvötn* caldera and built up a massive mountain ridge underneath the glacier. 5.000m³/s of 18°C hot water flowed down to the *Grímsvötn caldera*.

On the morning of 5th of November 1996, a 50.000 m³/s flood burst out at many places along the margin of the *Skeiðarárjökull* glacier and on to the bordering sands. The curve in the main road at *Gýgjukvísl* river resembles a dam, where the suction force of the water on the lee side has eroded the land, leaving a ledge of several metres height.

The main road ends just past the roadsign. The roaring flood torrent in background.

Looking across the centre of the town in the *Westman Islands* one year after the close of the eruption in July 1974. The new *Eldfell*, visible in the picture, buried the eastern part of the town - 400 houses – in ash and lava, the eruption lasting five months. The town is being excavated from the ash, but the upper parts and the harbour area have still not been cleared.

Katla in the *Mýrdals- jökull* glacier. Eruptions in the caldera are some- times huge and more powerful than other eruptions in Iceland. Eruption in *Katla* has been expected now for many years.

THE SOUTH

The South is an area of great contrasts. The largest lowland area in the country today is formed by what was the sea floor during the Ice Age. The coast is an almost unbroken 400 km stretch of pitch-black sandy beach.

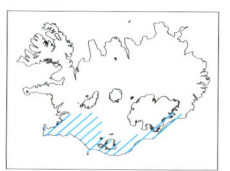

The South is the one area of Iceland where there are no true fjords. This has not always been the case and it is believed that at the end of the Ice Age the coast was cut by several fjords. At the close of the last glacial period when the glaciers were disappearing from the lowland, glacial rivers transported great amounts of sand and gravel to the sea. Large glacial rivers flow from *Vatnajökull* to *Skeiðarársandur*. Some originate from meltwater lakes at the edge of the glacier while others originate beneath the glacier itself. Under certain conditions great floods, so-called *jökulhlaup*, occur. Many of the largest *jökulhlaups* originate in *Grímsvötn*, which is a central volcano underneath *Vatnajökull*, where there is a lake covered by 200 m of ice. Geothermal heat at the bottom of the caldera melts the ice and causes the water level to rise. This enables the surrounding glacial ice to float with the result that the water bursts out from beneath and emerges as a *jökulhlaup* at the snout of the glacier. When the flood is at its height the discharge can greatly exceed that of the world's greatest river, the *Amazon* in Brazil. The lowlands of the South were at one time beneath the sea due to a higher world sea level. Beautiful mountains abound in the South, including *Hekla*, *Eyjafjallajökull* and *Tindfjöll*.

Hekla towers over the southern lowlands. The top crater is clearly visible.

The landscape west of *Hekla*. The moss grown lavas, from the major eruption of 1947 have almost buried the hills visible in the centre.

The summit crater on *Hekla*. It has erupted at least 24 times since the Settlement.

Lava tongues on the southwest flanks of *Hekla* from the eruption in 1991.

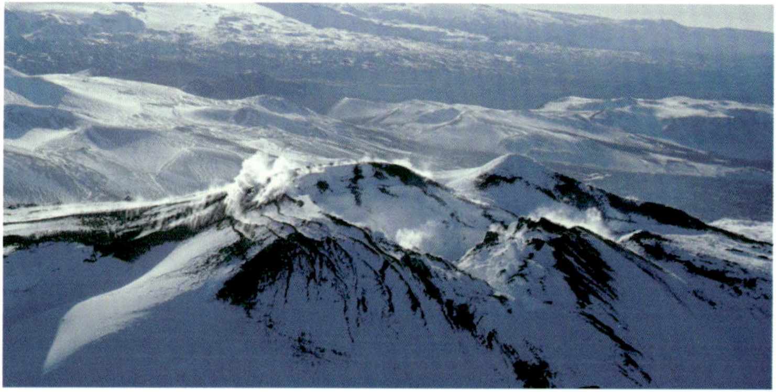

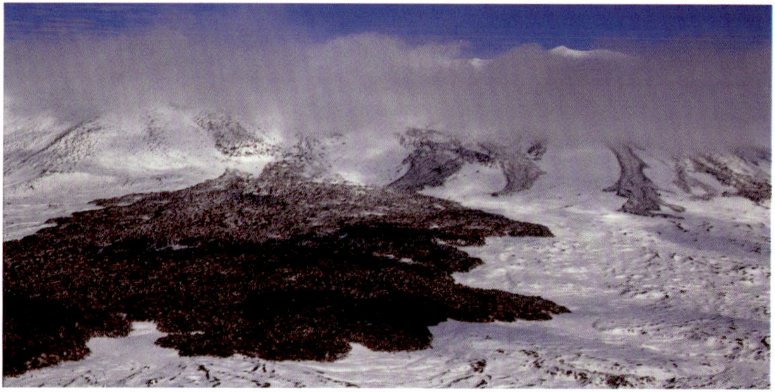

Dyrhólaey and *Reynishverfi* in *Mýrdal* are in the southernmost part of the country. *Dyrhólaey* is a 120 m high headland formed by the remains of a volcano which erupted in the last glacial period. The headland is a natural treasure and attracts large numbers of puffins and fulmars.

Looking across *Reynishverfi* in *Mýrdal*. *Katla* and *Mýrdalsjökull* visible in the background.

Eldey is the remains of a submarine volcano off the *Reykjanes* peninsula. Around 16.000 pairs of gannets nest on the rock.

Heimaey in the *Vestmannaeyjar* group looking towards the "mainland".

Surtsey and *Vestmannaeyjar*. *Surtsey* was formed during eruptions in the years 1963-1967.

Pages 42/43: Aerial view northwards across the island *Álsey*. The west coast of *Heimaey* in the background.

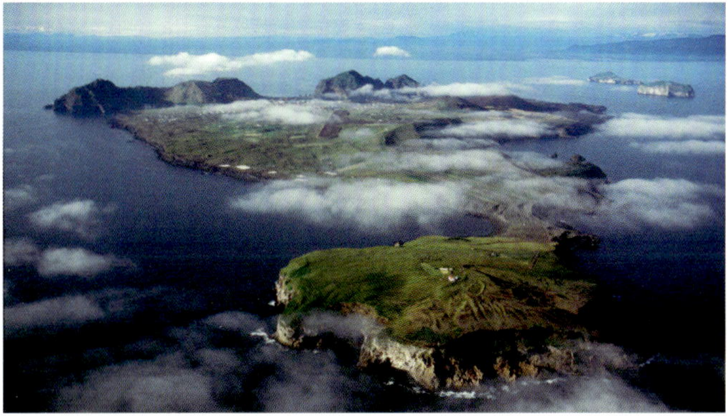

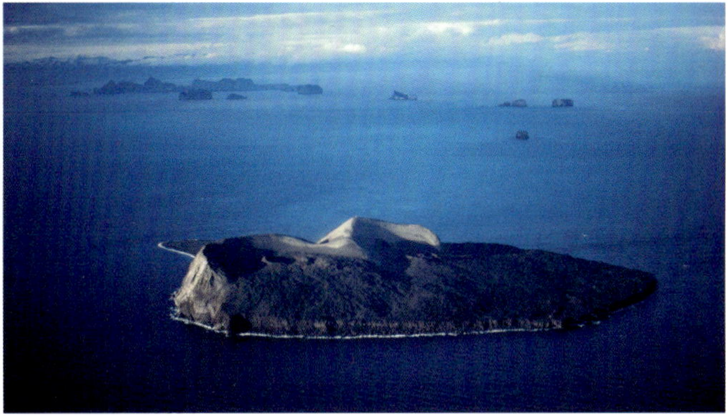

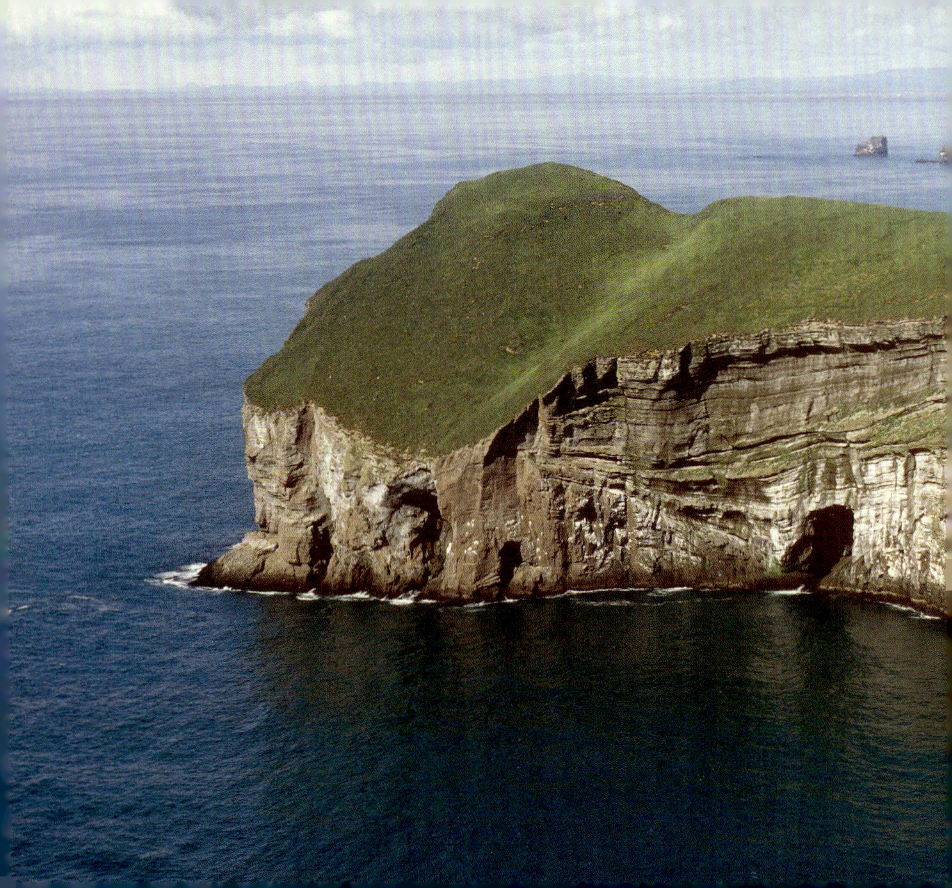

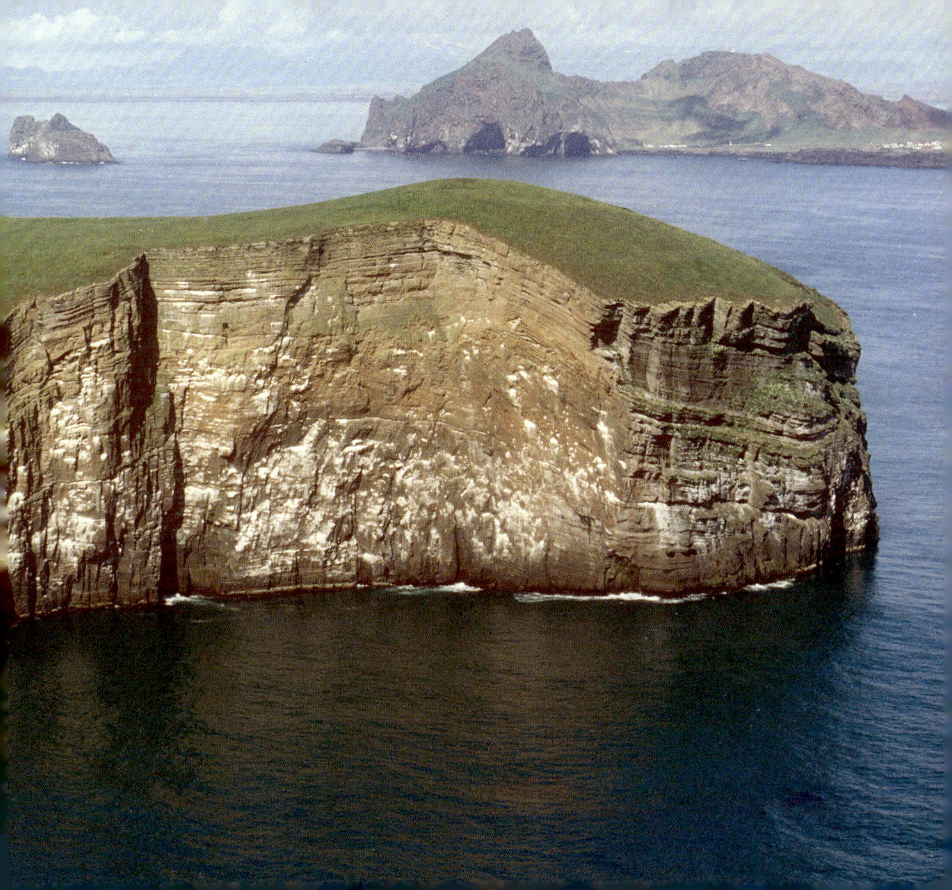

En echelon fractures on the western edge of Þingvellir rift valley. Here the European and N-American plates diverge.

Þingvellir is the cradle of democracy in western Europe. The parliament - Althingi - was founded in the year 930.

Fractures extend far out on the lake bottom.

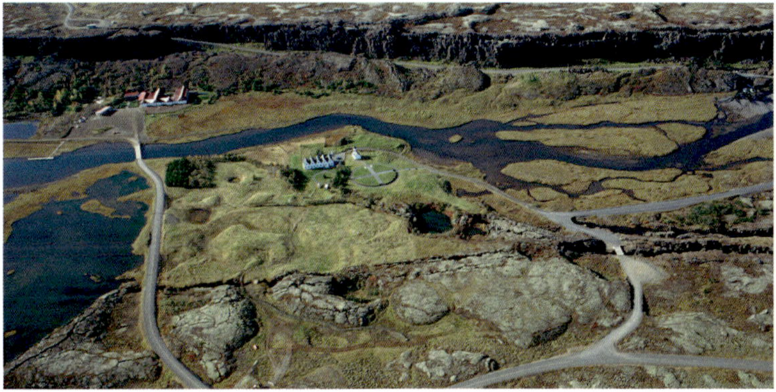

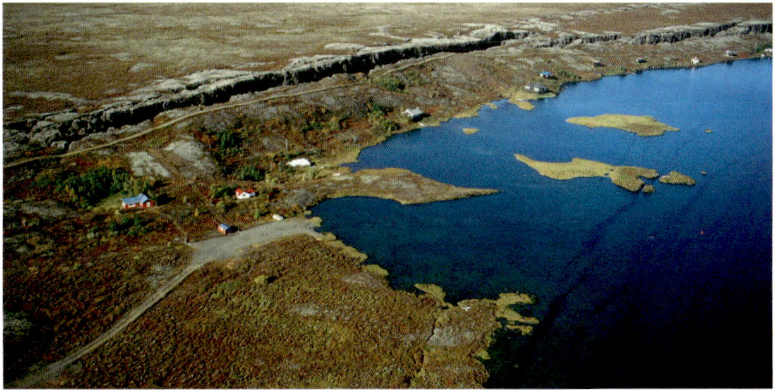

Gullfoss on *Hvítá* is one of the most magnificent waterfalls in the country.

View across part of the *Geysir* area. Old *Geysir* at lower right. *Strokkur* is erupting. According to sources, the history of hot spring eruptions at *Geysir* goes back to the earthquakes in the southern lowlands of 1294.

Large rivers from *Vatnajökull* flow in numerous braided channels over the sands at *Skeiðarársandur* which represent the largest expanse of their type in the country at almost 1000 sq.km. The sands consist of the glaciofluvial sediment of the rivers from *Skeiðarárjökull,* in particular flood waters from the *Grænalón* ice-dammed lake and recently of the *Grímsvötn* floods during November 1996. Further inland *Lómagnúpur* rises almost 700 metres above the western part of the sands. In the glow of the setting sun the water channels become ribbons of gold and silver.

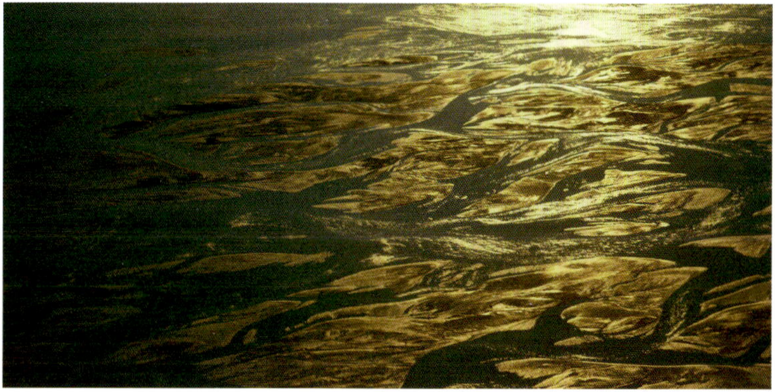

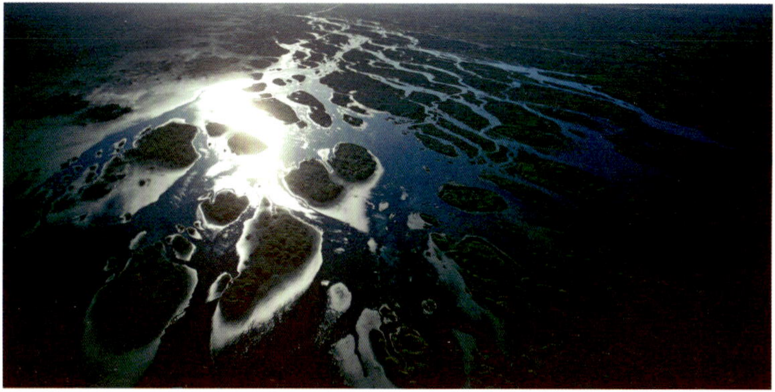

Icebergs calving from the margin of *Breiðamerkurjökull* (see also photo overleaf) float in the *Jökulsárlón* and eventually reach the sea. *Jökulsárlón* is the deepest lake in the country, with a depth of 260 metres excavated by the constant erosion of the moving *Breiðamerkurjökull* valley glacier in the distance.

Skarðatindur and *Kristínartindar* southeast of *Morsárjökull*.

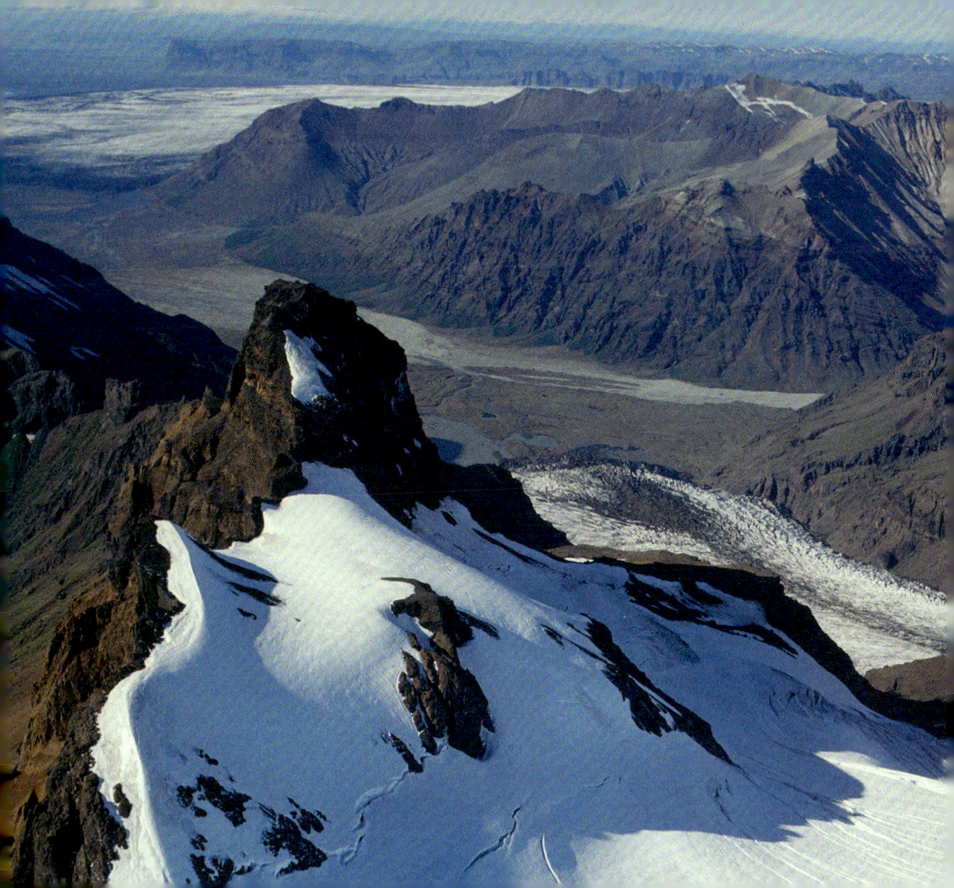

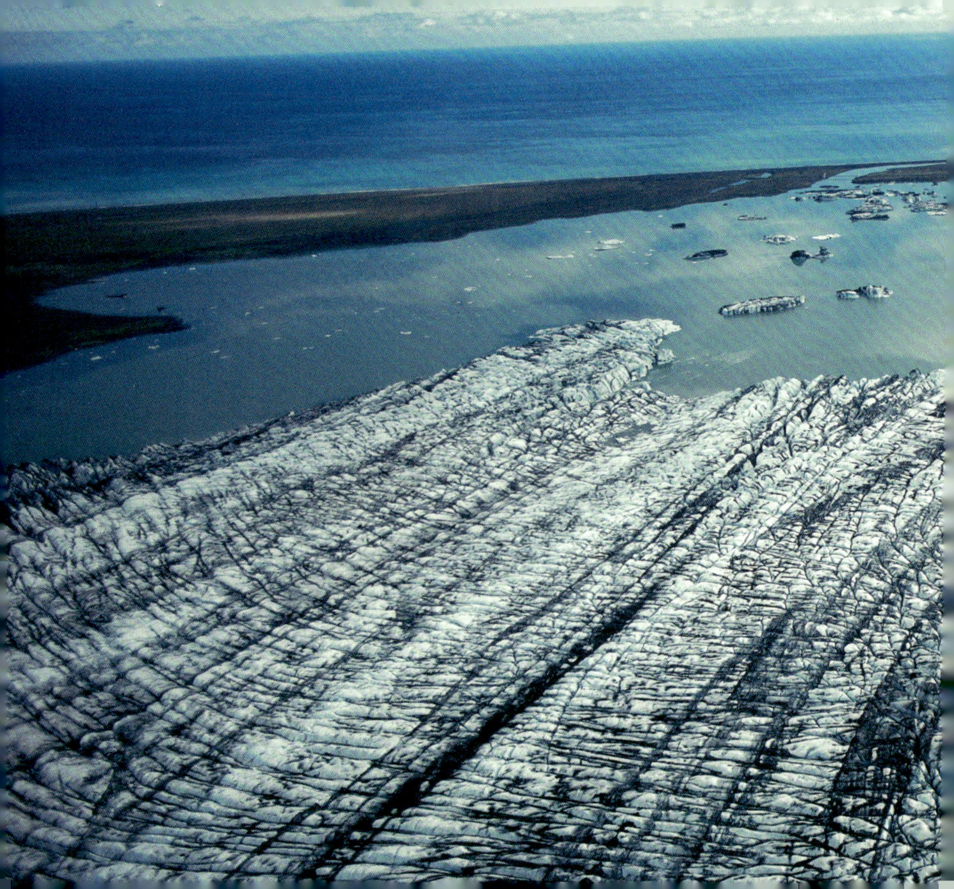

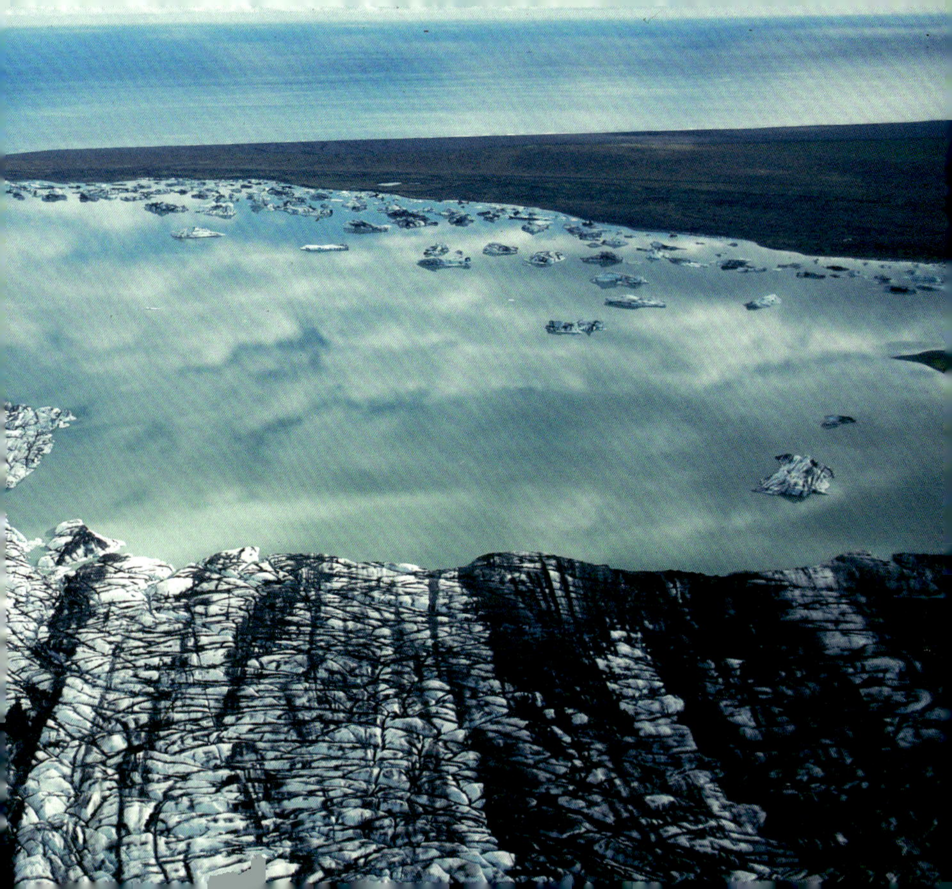

Thin snowcover in early autumn at *Fögrufjöll* -
"Mountains of Beauty". River *Skaftá* in foreground.

Crevasses form on the glacier when it slides
over rock barriers in its path (*Goðalandsjökull* in *Þórsmörk*).

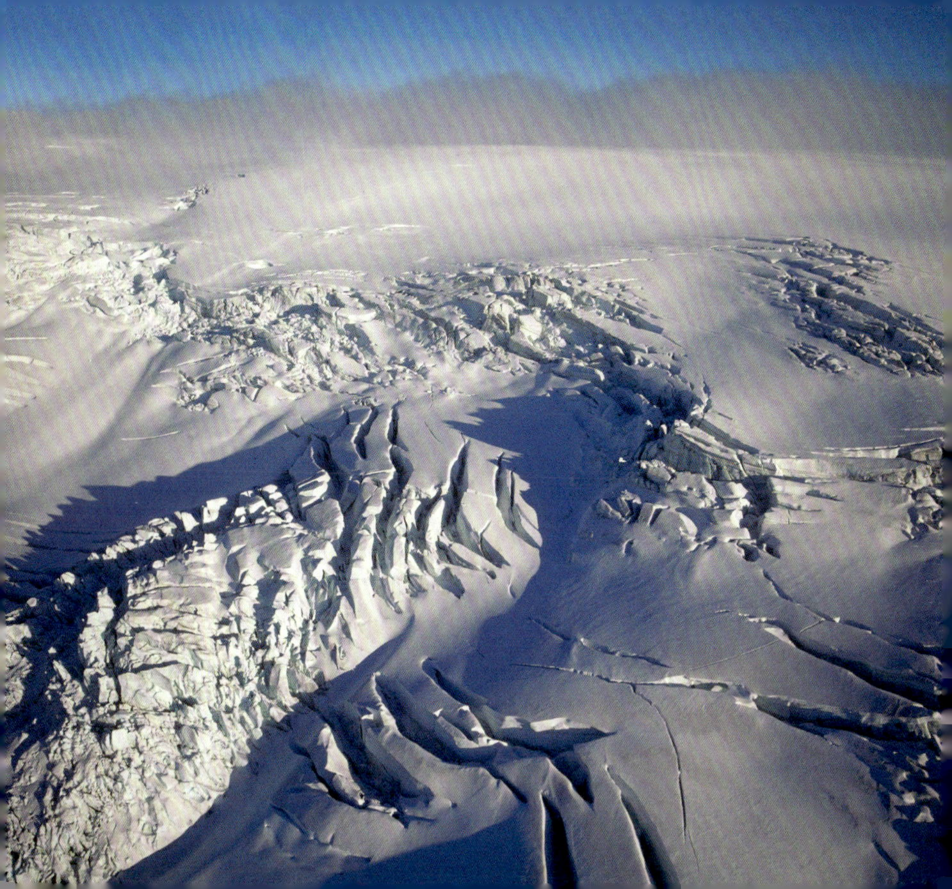

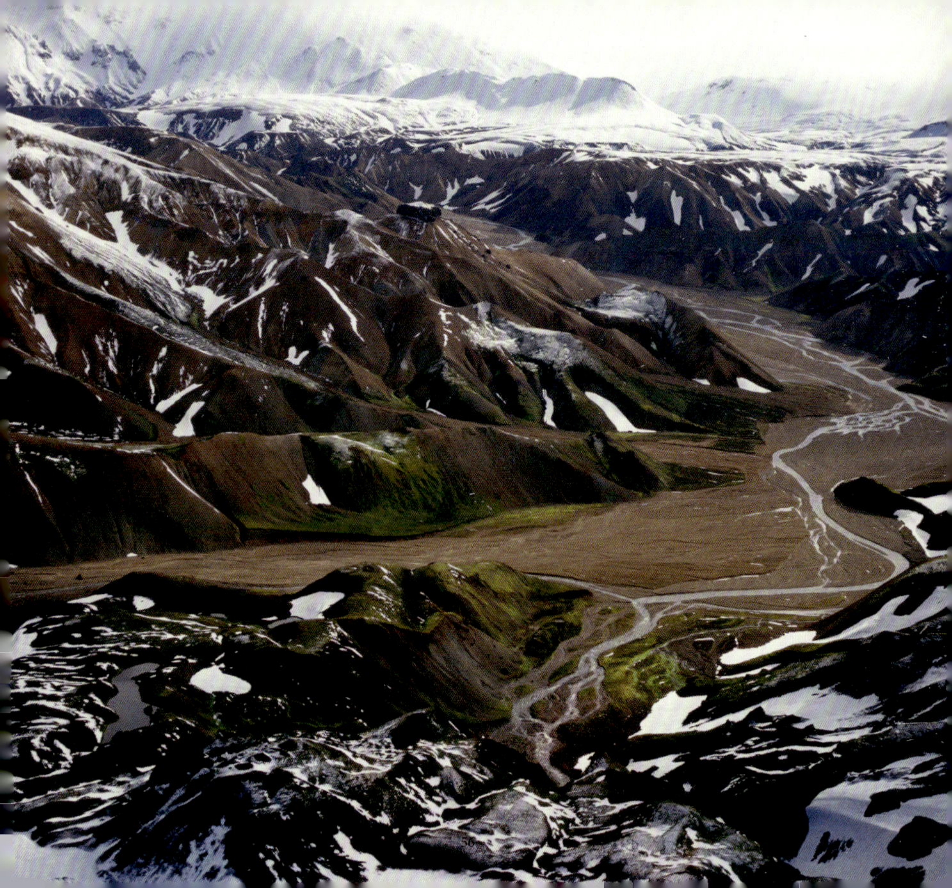

SOUTHERN HIGHLANDS

Light green moss extends up the mountain sides. In *Landmannalaugar* the rocks display all the colours of the rainbow. At *Laki* the craters are moss grown and some contain blue-green tarns. Together this conveys the magnificent grandeur of nature.

Along the centre of southern Iceland lies an upland area which runs from *Hekla* eastwards to *Vatnajökull*. This upland area is often known as the Southern Highlands. There are many central volcanoes and eruptive vents, craters and fissures which are almost impossible to count. Many unique oases of vegetation occur in this area. In the *Landmannalaugar* region the rhyolite displays all the colours of the rainbow. Compounds of iron and other metals result in a variety of colours in the rock as well as yellow which is the most common, there is red, blue-green, green, pink and pure black rock. North of *Landmannalaugar* are crater rows which extend far inland towards *Vatnajökull*. At *Lakagígar* there is a row of about 135 craters which were formed in a large eruption in 1783. Stories of the eruption evoke dread in most Icelanders. The lava is one of the most extensive to have erupted on earth during historical times, its gas emission having highly destructive consequences. But in just over two hundred years the craters at *Laki* have evolved into a true work of art. In many of them there are blue green tarns while beautiful dwarf shrubs thrive in the shelter of the crater walls. Where the forces of nature once posed the worst possible threat, there now exists perfect shelter for even the most delicate forms of life.

In *Landmannalaugar*, *Jökulgil* sweeps upwards to the foot of *Torfajökull*.

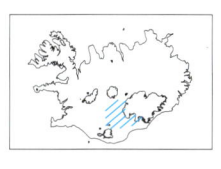

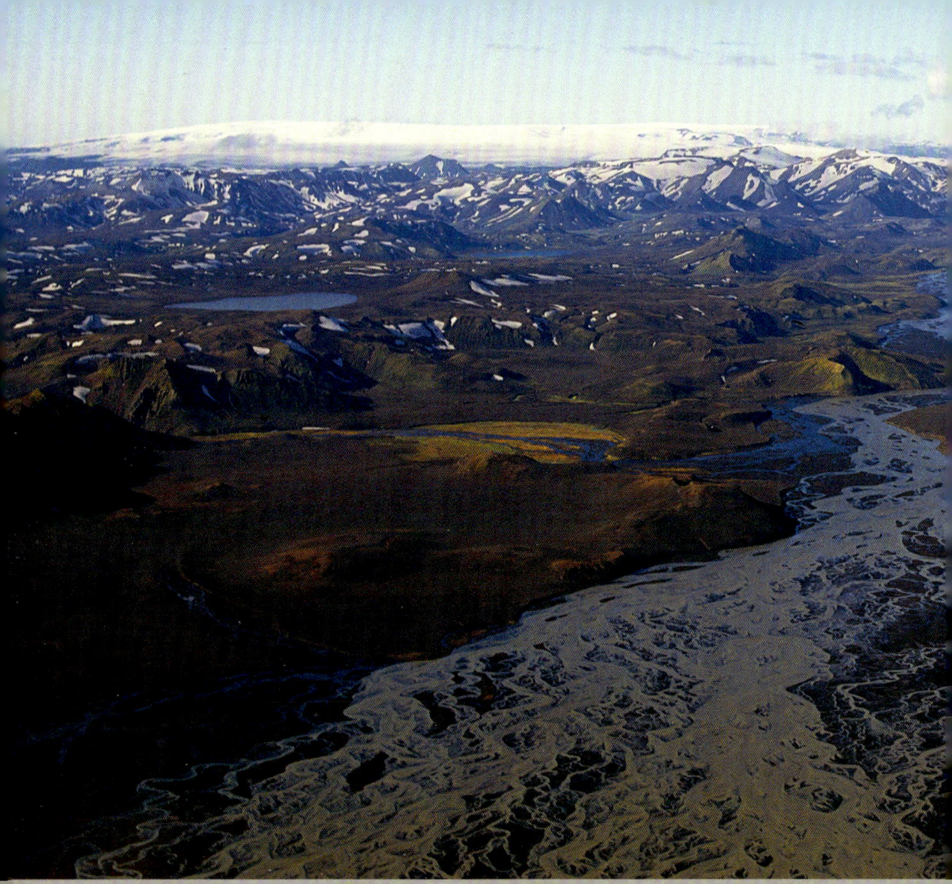

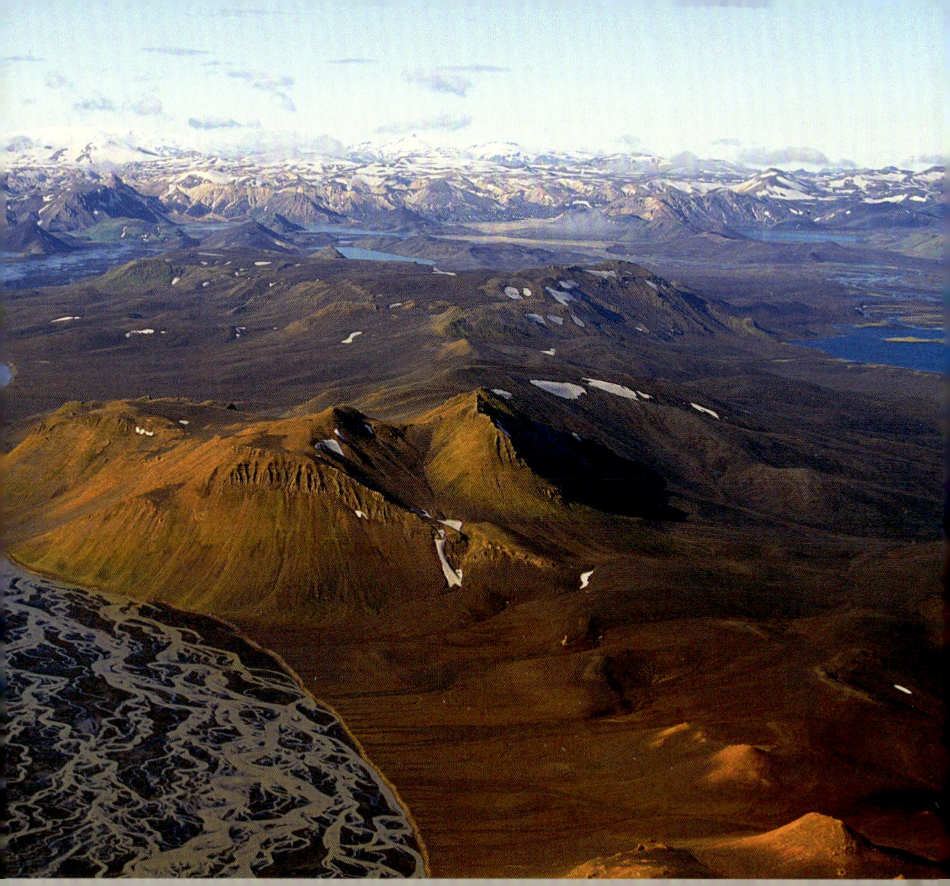

Looking out along *Jökulgil* towards *Landmannalaugar* and *Laugahraun*.

Laugahraun lava erupted about 500 years ago.

Pages 58/59: Looking westwards along the course of the *Tungnaá*.
On the horizon *Katla* is visible on the left and *Eyjafjallajökull* just right of centre.

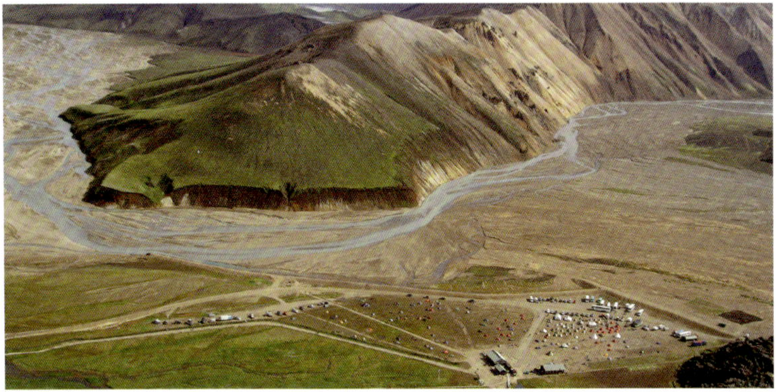

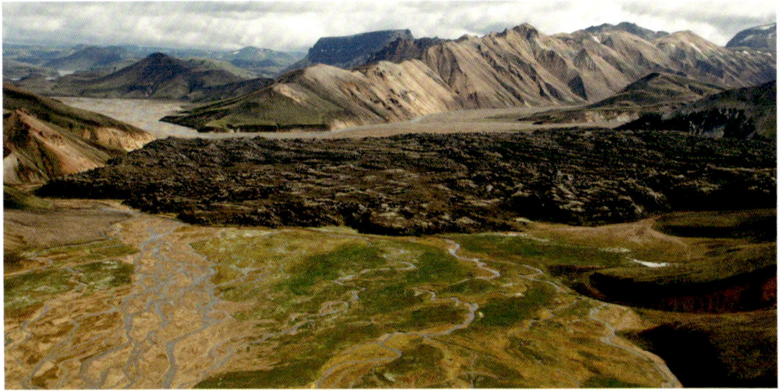

Narrow sharp edged slopes furthest up
Jökulgil. Light coloured rhyolite characterises the landscape.

North of *Landmannalaugar* are *Frostastaðavatn*
(farthest right) and *Ljótipollur* (foreground left).

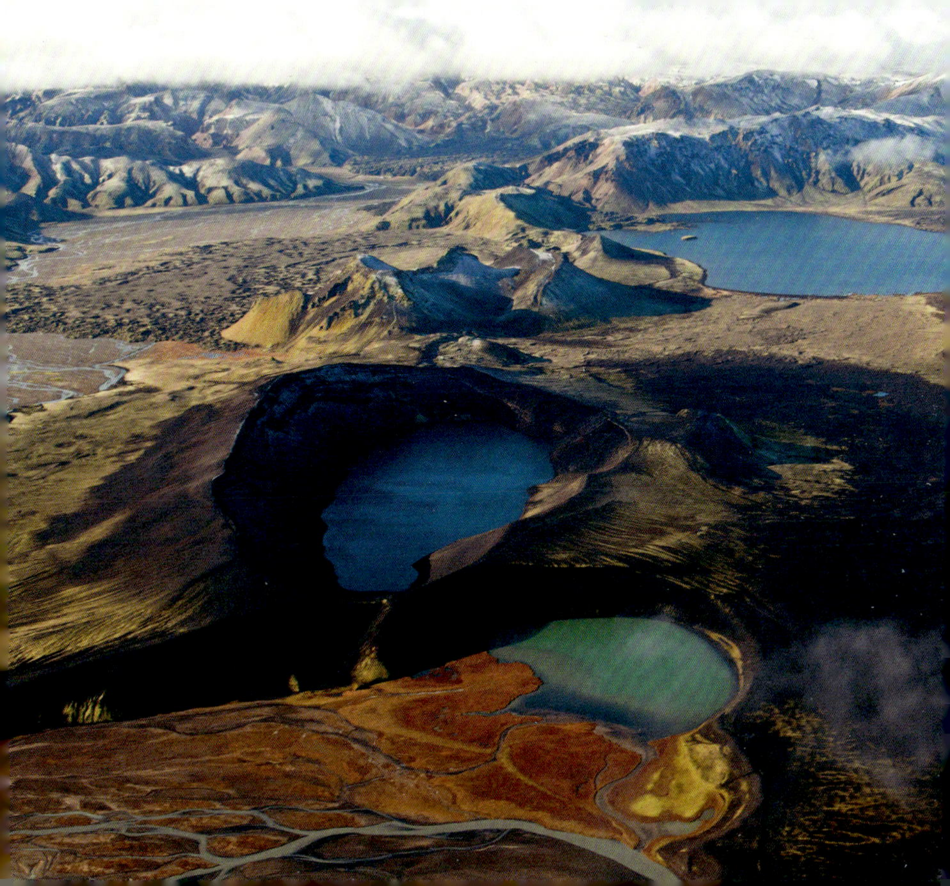

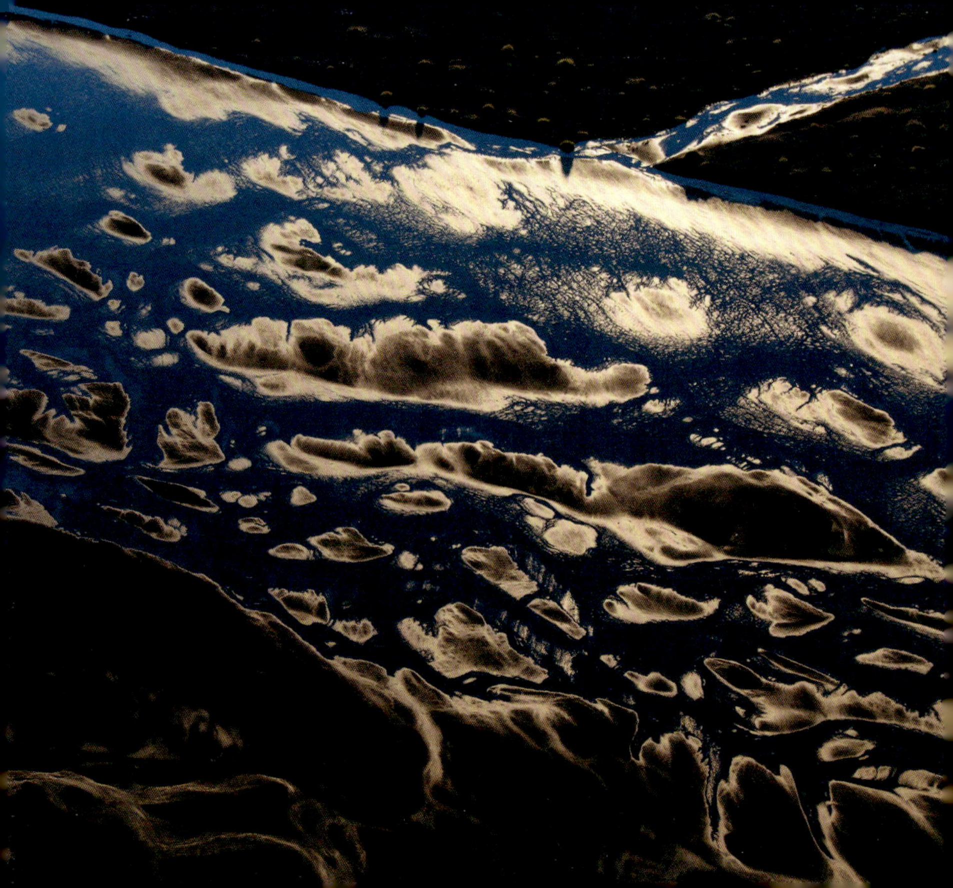

Sandbanks are widespread in mountain
rivers just as on the lowlands, where
the land is flat and the river velocity decreases.

Craters and craterlike forms at *Fögrufjöll* -
"Mountains of Beauty" - at Lake *Langisjór*.

At *Laki* there are around 135 craters on a 25 km long eruption fissure. One of the largest and widely felt eruptions in the history of Iceland and in World's history, it began in the early summer of 1783 and lasted for eight months with the result that in the following years about one fifth of the population died as well as the largest part of the agricultural livestock.

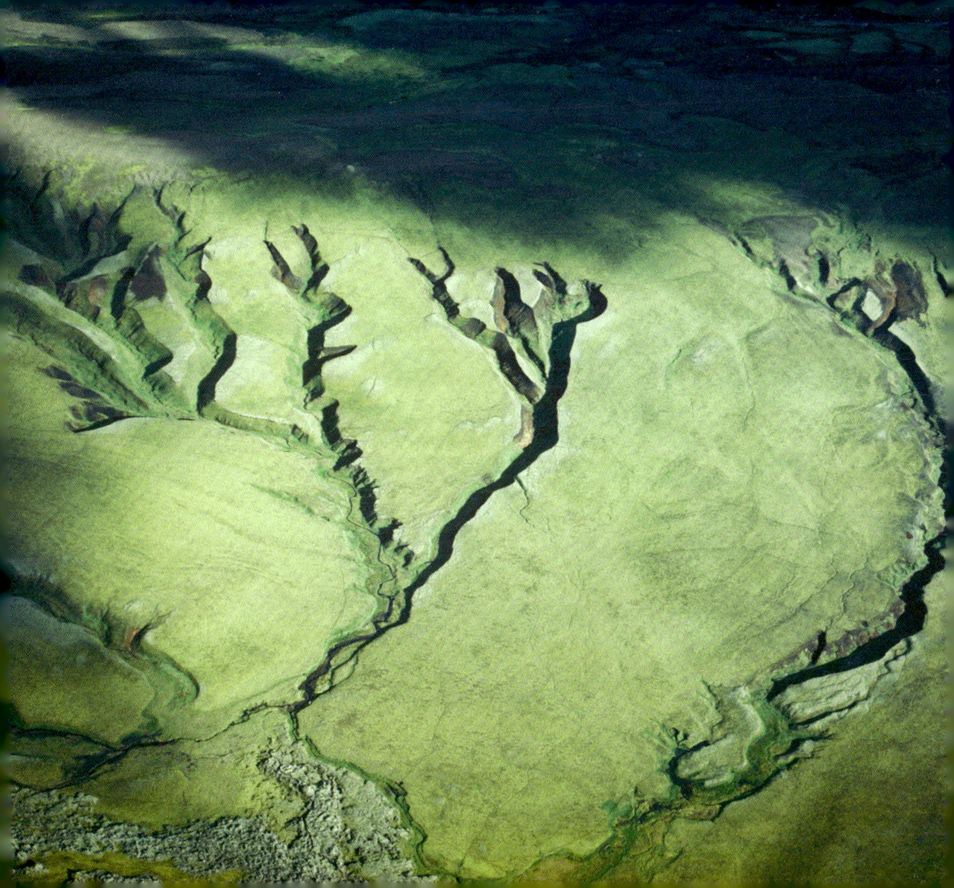

Evening sun lights up the rhyolite rocks at *Barmur* at *Landmannalaugar*.

Water eroded channels along a ridge in the innermost part of *Jökulgil* in *Landmannalaugar*.

Page 67: Creek channels ornamenting the land at *Skaftártungur*.

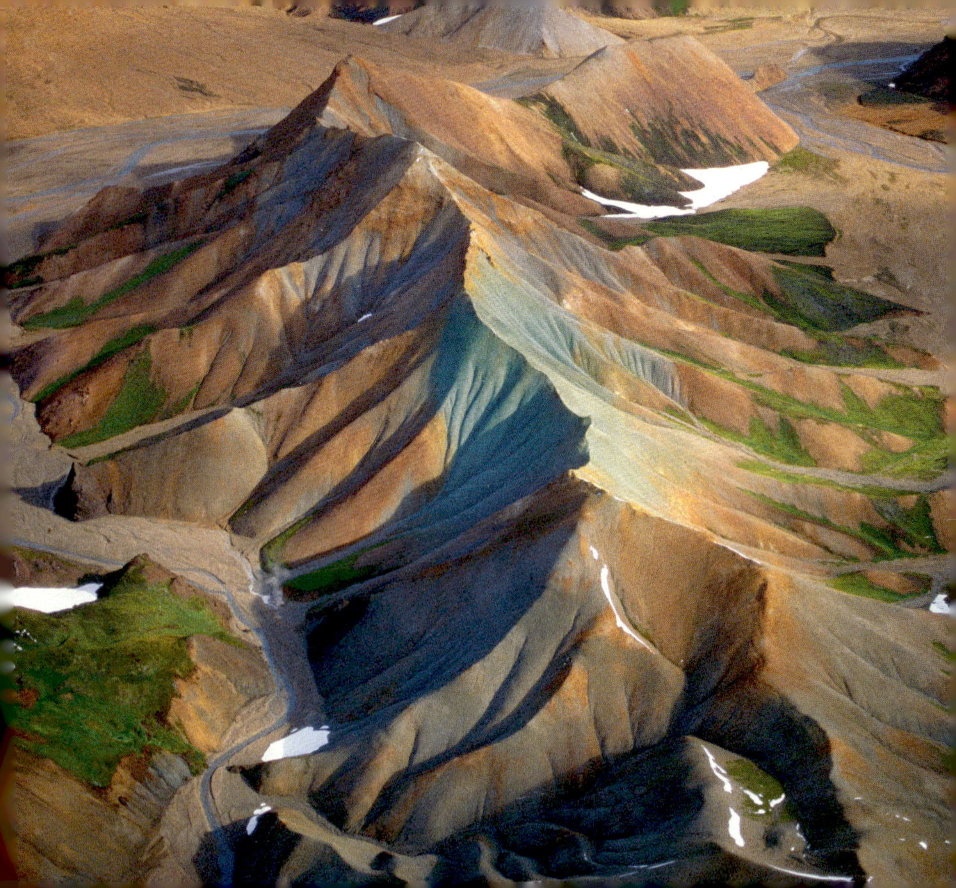

A dusting of snow crowns one of the *Laki* craters in autumn.

A lava field between the *Laki* crater row and *Fögrufjöll*.
Groundwater, sediment and moss decorate the surface.

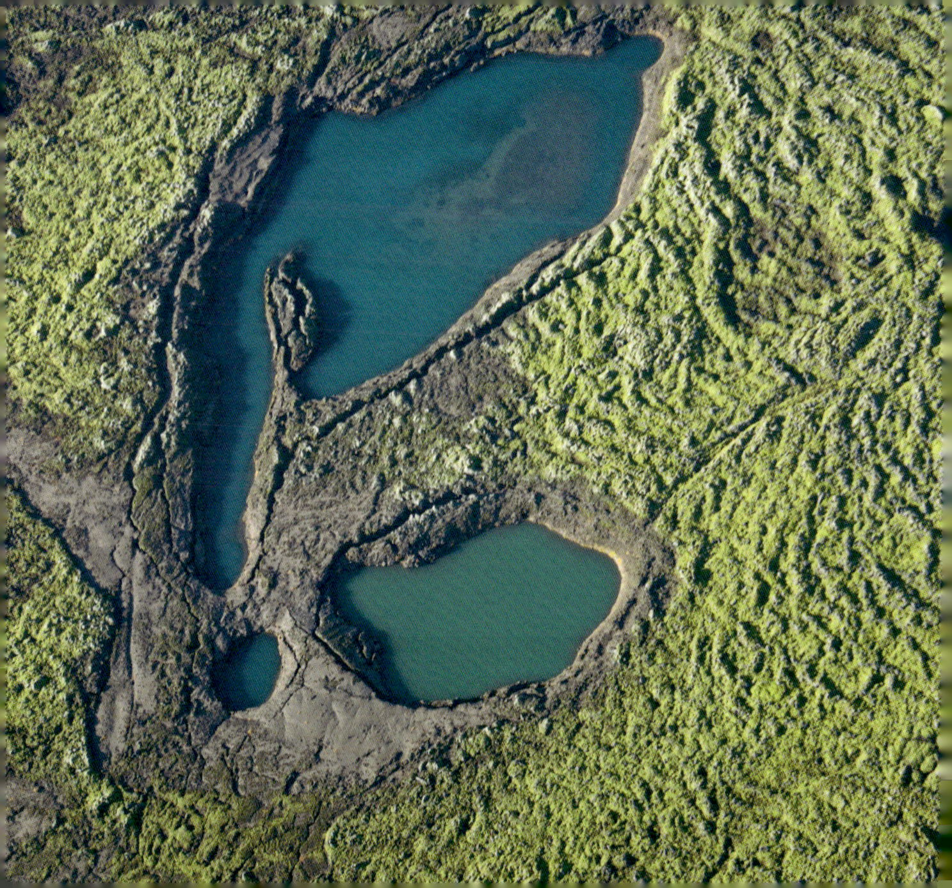

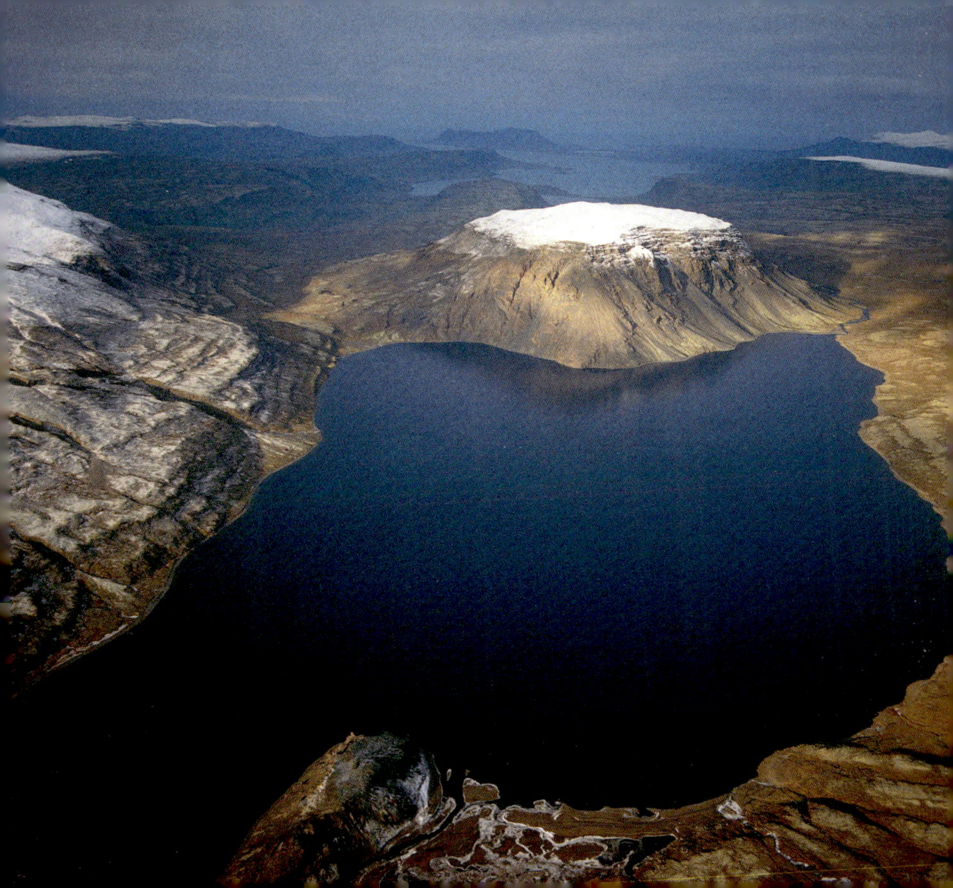

THE WEST

On the *Snæfellsnes* peninsula there are long beaches of golden shelly sand. There are also many unusual craters and lavas. In *Breiðafjörður* and *Hvammsfjörður* there are islands and skerries by the thousand. Luxuriant growth typifies *Borgarfjörður*, while majestic mountains dominate the landscape.

Glacial erosion typifies much of the landscape in the West. Over wide areas glaciers have succeeded in eroding the land down to sea level. Examples of this are *Borgarfjörður* and *Mýrar*. Surrounding the area are majestic mountains which have been partly dissected by glaciers, an example of which is *Skarðsheiði* encircling *Borgarfjörður* to the south.

Rocky hills and cliffs characterise to a great extent the landscape of *Borgarfjörður*, giving way to extensive moorlands further inland where there are countless mountain tarns and many bogs. In most of the lakes there are trout and varied and abundant birdlife on the moors. From the highland inland of the moors rises the 1675 m high *Eiríksjökull*, a large table mountain capped by a dome shaped glacier.

Snæfellsnes lies furthest west in the region. Many small volcanoes can be found on the peninsula. One is *Eldborg* in *Hnappadalur*, a spatter cone of around 7000 years old, one of three on a short fissure. A number of lavas have flowed radially from *Snæfellsjökull*, some of them into the sea, especially to the south and west. The youngest flows are only 1800 years old.

Hvalvatn is a natural extension of *Hvalfjörður*, blocked by *Hvalfell*.

Hraunsfjörður on northern *Snæfellsnes* in late winter sunlight.

Overleaf: The summit of *Snæfellsjökull* (1446 m). Countless lavas shape the western and southern slopes of the volcano. Some lavas are 1800 years old.

Lake *Skorradalsvatn* in *Borgarfjörður*
is situated in a long glacially eroded valley. *Hlöðufell* (see page 127)
visible on the horizon below white cloud left of centre background.

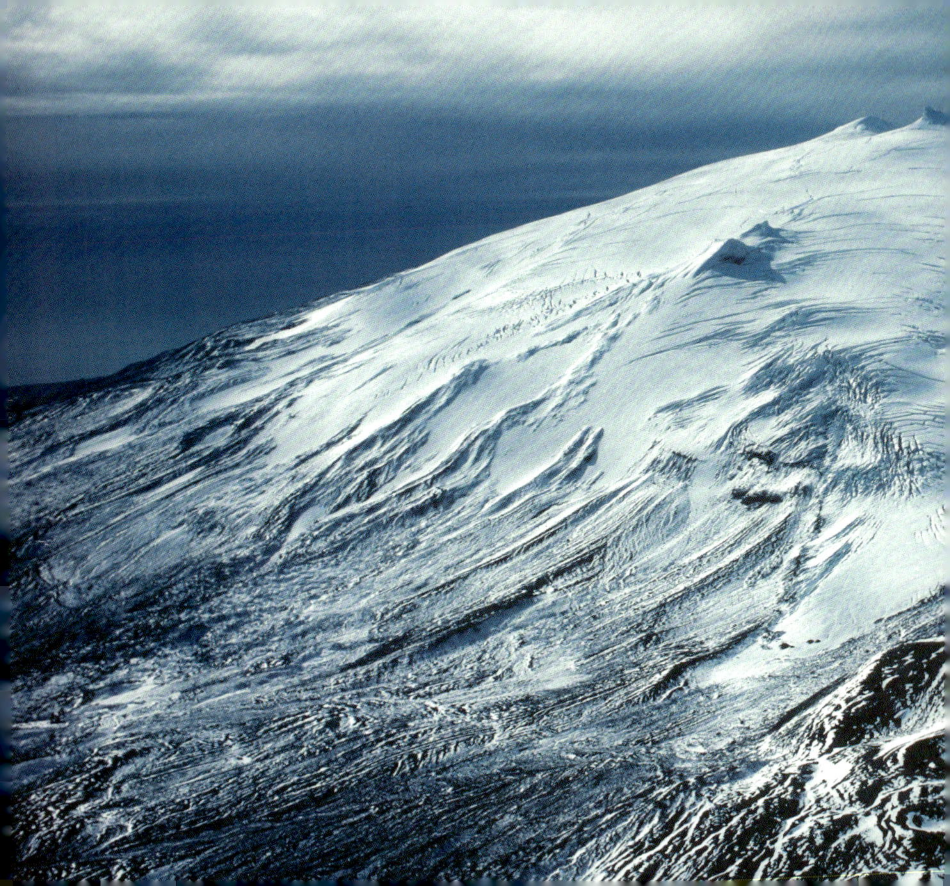

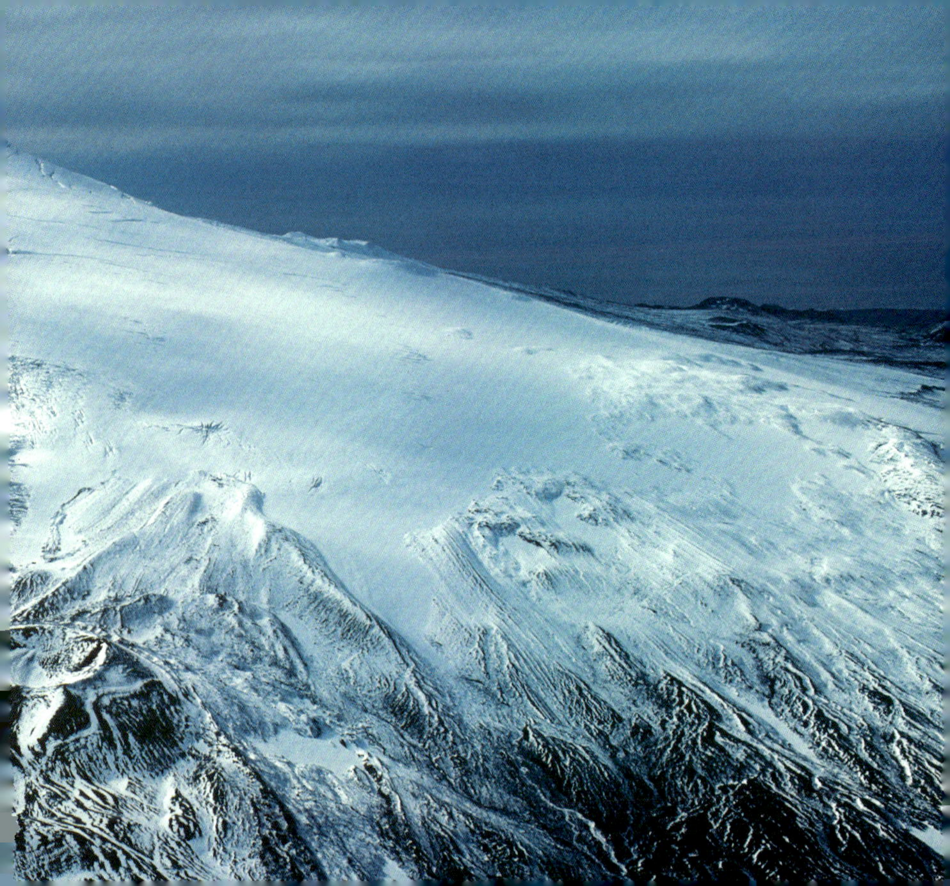

Eldborg in *Hnappadalur* is one of the most beautifully shaped craters in the country. The eruption occurred some 5-7000 years ago.

Skarðsheiði borders the southern part of *Borgarfjörður*.

Tröllakirkja above *Hítardalur* and *Mýrar*. The peak is composed of old lavas.

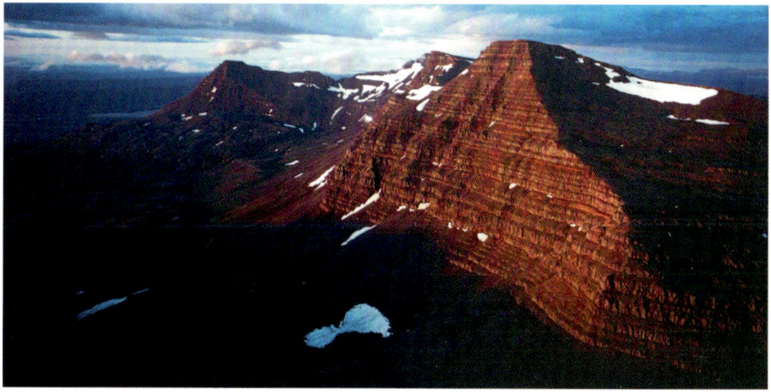

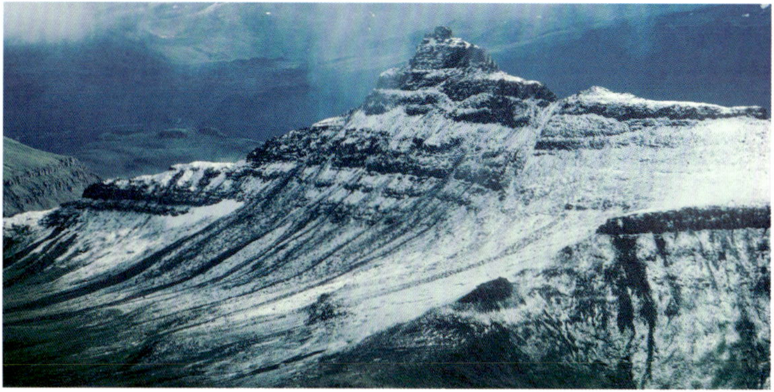

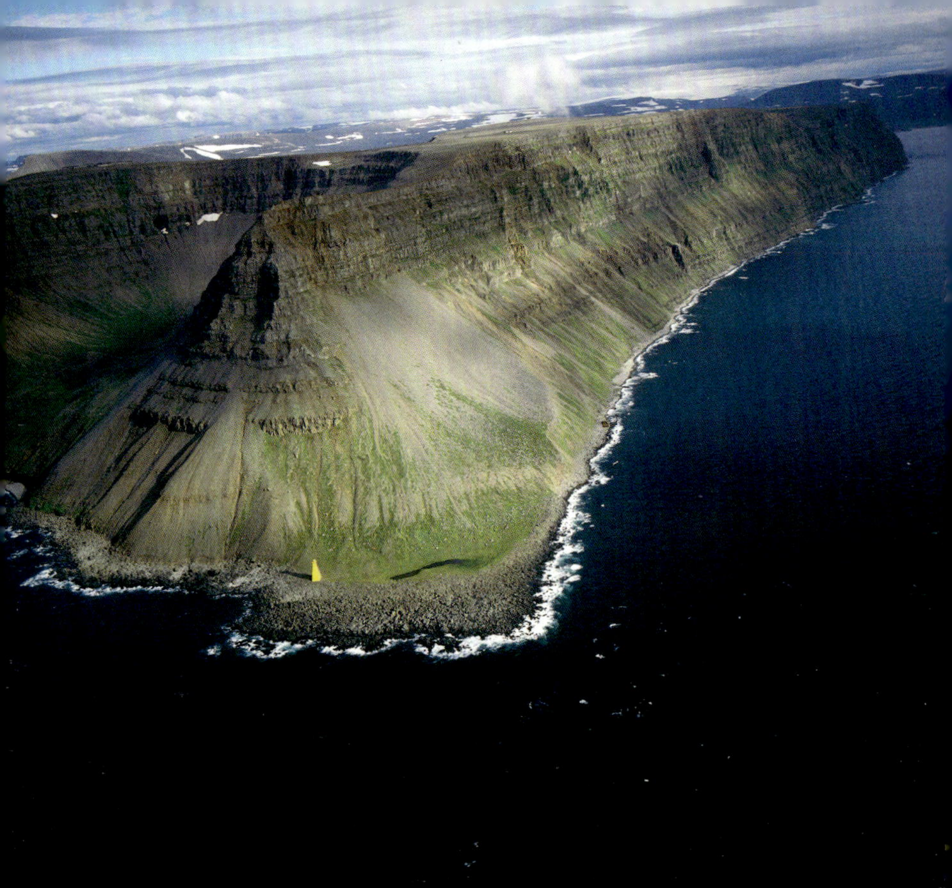

THE WESTERN FJORDS

Three of the largest bird-nesting cliffs in Iceland are located in the Western Fjords. One of them, *Látrabjarg*, is 441 metres high and well over fourteen kilometres in length. The largest nature reserve in the country is at *Hornstrandir*, a sanctuary for plants and animals.

As in the East, some of Iceland's oldest geological formations are found in the Western Fjords. It has been about fifteen million years since this area was formed from eruptions along the Mid-Atlantic Ridge. Since then the Western Fjords have been drifting to the northwest with the North-American plate. Millions of years have passed since these volcanoes were active and with the passage of time any traces of lava and craters on the surface have disappeared.

With the onset of the Ice Age, glacial erosion became dominant in shaping the landscape of the Western Fjords, although some mountain peaks were ice free. By the end of that era the erosive powers of the glaciers were almost sufficient to separate the Western Fjords from the rest of the country. *Drangajökull*, one of Iceland's five major glaciers, is here, and its very existence expresses the harsh weather of this area better than any words. A surprisingly short distance, or only 285 km, separates Greenland from the Western fjords. During the late winter, drift ice from Greenland sometimes reaches the Western Fjords. The southern coast of the region is indented by numerous fjords while myriads of islands and skerries lie offshore.

Straumnesfjall
at *Hornstrandir*, one of several promontories in the Western Fjords.

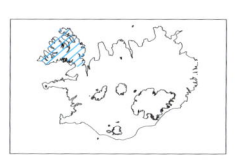

Látrabjarg is one of the largest bird cliffs in the country. Here it rises 440 metres up from the sea. Great numbers of guillemots, cormorants, kittiwakes and puffins nest on the cliffs. One of Iceland's most daring sea-rescue operations took place at *Látrabjarg* in December 1947, when local farmers rescued 12 of 15 crewmembers from the stranded trawler Dhoon, hoisting the men several hundred metres up the treacherous ice-covered cliffs to safety.

Kögur is one of the magnificent
promontories in the northwest region of *Hornstrandir*.

Sandoddi in *Patreksfjörður*. The sand spit is composed of golden shelly sand.

Landforms of great beauty develop
where the sea flows in and out of a lagoon at *Rauðisandur*.

Rauðisandur with its
yellow-peach colour is one of the most extensive beaches in the Western Fjords.

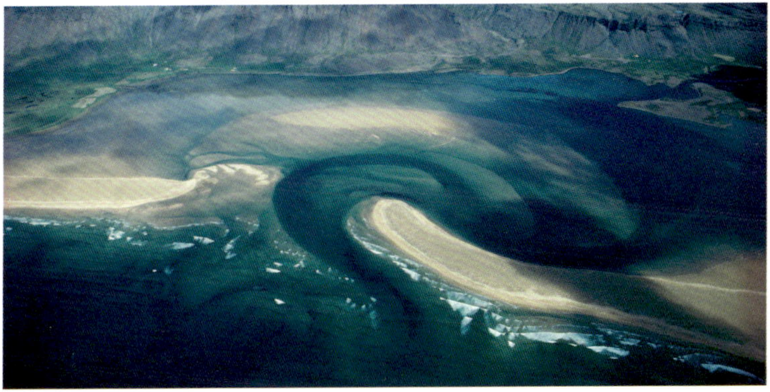

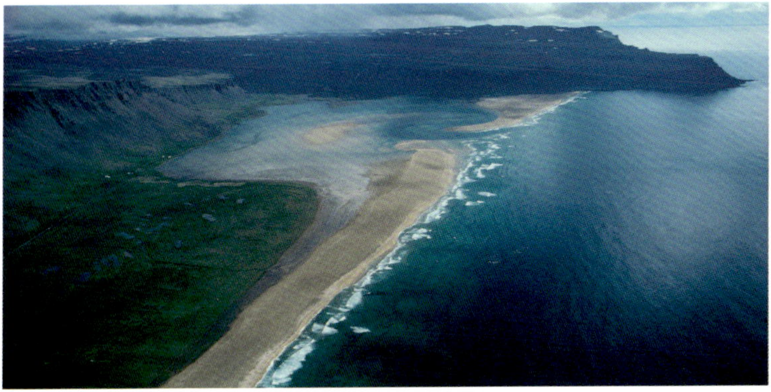

Evening beauty at *Dýrafjörður*,
one of the southern fjords in the Western Fjords region.

Skáleyjar is one of the largest island groups in *Breiðafjörður*.

Vigur is an island in *Ísafjarðadjúp*. It has the only wind-powered corn mill in the country. The oldest information sources about habitation on *Vigur* are from 1194.

The cliffs at *Drangaskörð* rise magnificently to face the sea at *North-Strandir*.

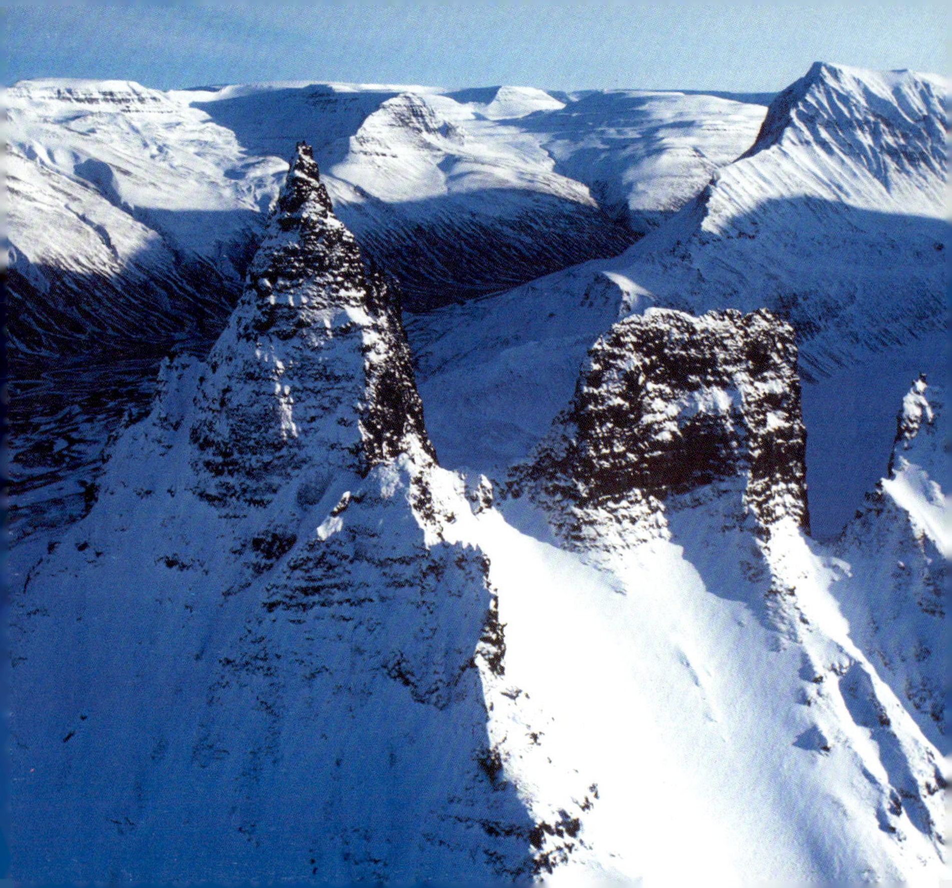

THE NORTH

The North presents a varied landscape. Pleasantly sheltered valleys beneath high mountains, moorlands covered in lakes and tarns, peninsulas which are often highland or lowland, broad bays and black sandy coasts, marshland and islands off the coast with seabird colonies.

The northern part of Iceland was formed at a similar time to the Western Fjords and the East. The oldest parts of the North are the promontories on either side of the seaward end of *Eyjafjörður*. The mountains in this area are the remains of the original lava pile which was formed about ten to twelve million years ago. Ice Age glaciers eroded the rocks and carried the resulting debris out onto the continental shelf. The valleys are mirror images of the mountains. They have formed where rivers and alpine glaciers have carved deep into the bedrock. There were unusually many alpine glaciers in the North during glacial periods and they have eroded a great many valleys, large and small. Most of the valleys are in *Skagafjörður* and *Eyjafjörður* where they are up to fifteen kilometres in width. The longest valleys are also found in this part of the country, of which *Bleiksmýrardalur* is a good example. Geographical conditions ensure that in the summer the North and East are relatively mild and conducive to growth. Mild southerly winds are dried and warmed adiabatically as they move northwards over the highland. The air becomes rapidly warmer on its way from the highlands down to the lowlands of the North. Northerly winds, however, produce cooler and drier air.

Hraundrangi rises majestically on the jagged edge between *two valleys*.

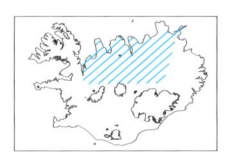

Hrísey, a beautifully shaped island in *Eyjafjörður*.
The island has a population of some 200 inhabitants.

Flatey is a quite large and completely flat island
lying a short distance offshore from *Húsavík* in *Skjálfandaflói*.

Auðkúluheiði is covered by Ice Age morainic deposits.
The river *Blanda* has carved its channel down through the lava pile.

Bleiksmýrardalur is one of the finest shaped
glacially eroded valleys in the country. During glacial periods a glacier
tongue extended for some 100 km from the interior of Iceland into the sea.

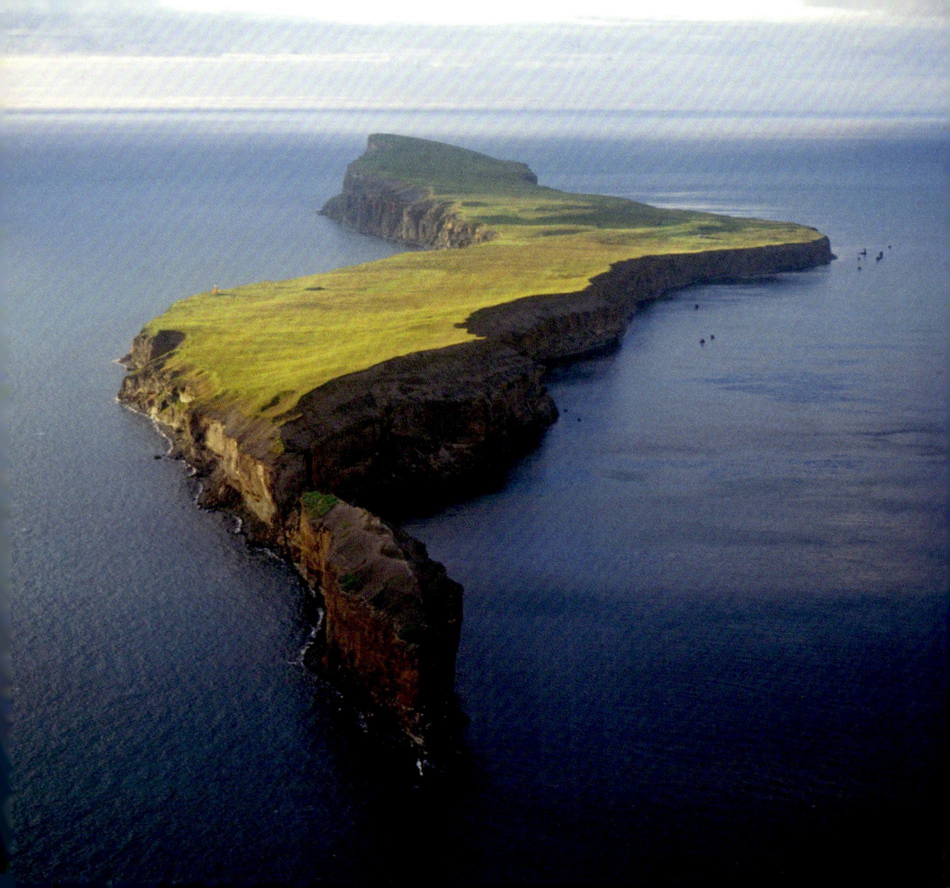

Málmey in *Skagafjörður* is a beautifully shaped island.
Settlement on *Málmey* ceased around the middle of the last century.

Thousands of birds gliding at the bird colony on the east of *Grímsey*.

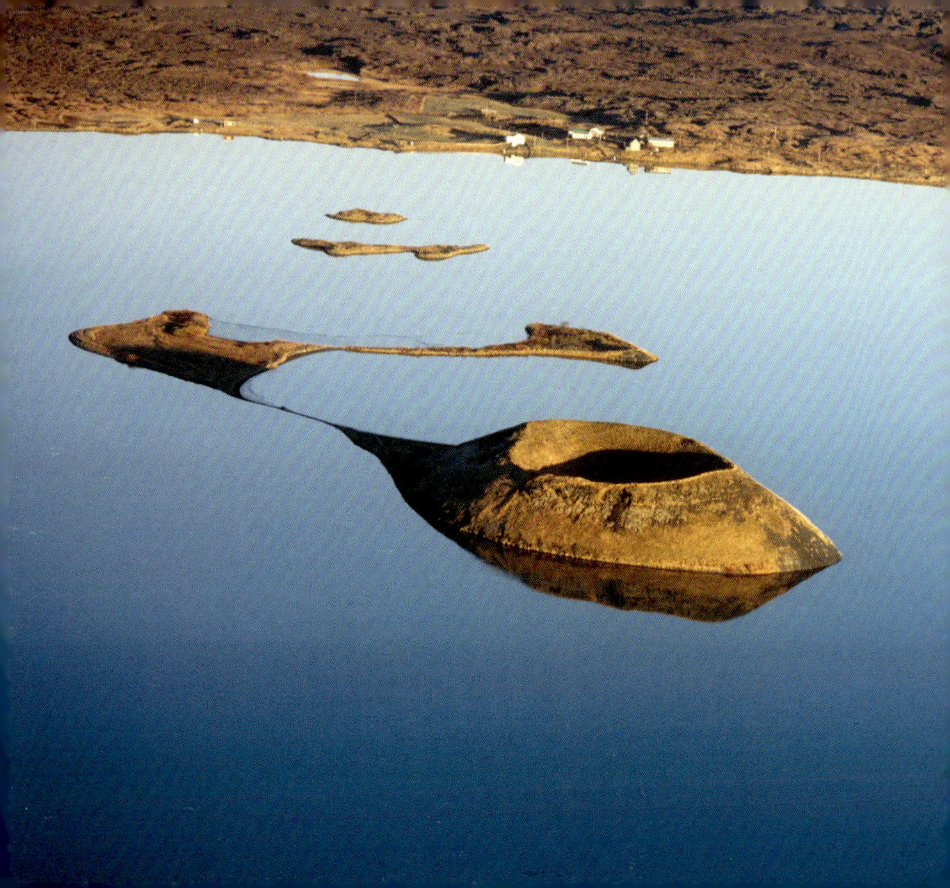

LAKE MÝVATN

Mother Nature has collected in one area many of Iceland's magnificent natural wonders. There are craters of all sizes and shapes, crater rows and many types of mountain. In addition the *Mývatn* area has some of the most unique plant and bird life in Iceland.

To the east of the highland of Northern Iceland the land becomes lower and the stark landscape gives way to rolling countryside. Here is *Mývatn*, one of the jewels of Icelandic nature. During the 10.000 years since the Ice Age, the landscape in this region has changed incredibly. By the end of the Ice Age the landscape around *Mývatn* may have been similar to the present day landscape in places along the edge of *Vatnajökull*. The glacial deposits gradually became weathered, a soil cover developed and in time vegetation took root.

There have been frequent eruptions in this region as it is located at the western margin of the northern volcanic zone. There were large lava eruptions to the south of *Mývatn* about 3800 years ago and again 1800 years ago. Lake *Mývatn* owes its present appearance largely to lava from this eruption. The islands in the lake as well as most of *Mývatn*'s environs were formed during this eruption. The islands, most of which are pseudocraters, formed as the lava flowed over the bogs or into the shallow lake. Water trapped by the red hot lava became superheated and consequent steam explosions caused the formation of the pseudocraters which are unlike the volcanic craters in not having magma feeding vents.

Autumn stillness at Lake *Mývatn*.

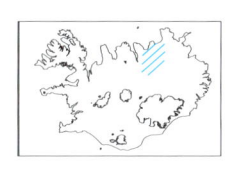

Looking northwest
across *Mývatn* on an autumn evening. Groups of pseudocraters
can be seen on the islands in the lake. *Vindbelgjarfjall* in the background.

It is thought that this unique formation at *Höfði* was
the result of lava flowing into *Mývatn* from the *Lúdentsborgir* and
Þrengslaborgir crater rows through the *Dimmuborgir* area just over 2000 years ago.

Hverfjall is a 2300 - 2800 year old explosion crater in *Mývatnssveit*.

At *Krafla* the land has become buried
in lava, but small outliers of land stand up here and there.

The *Krafla* area from an altitude of 4000 meters.
Viewed towards the north. Same angle as in photo above.

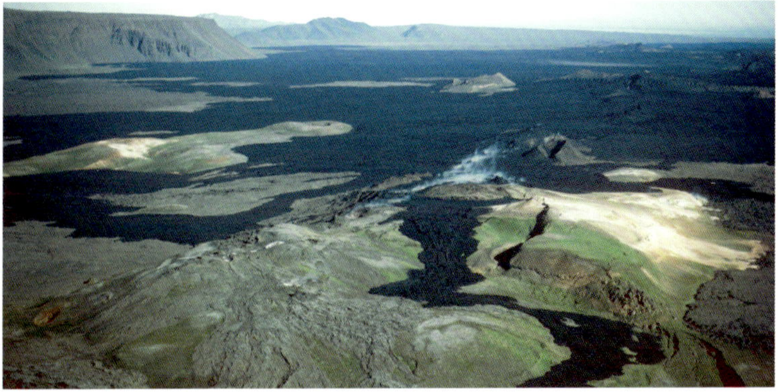

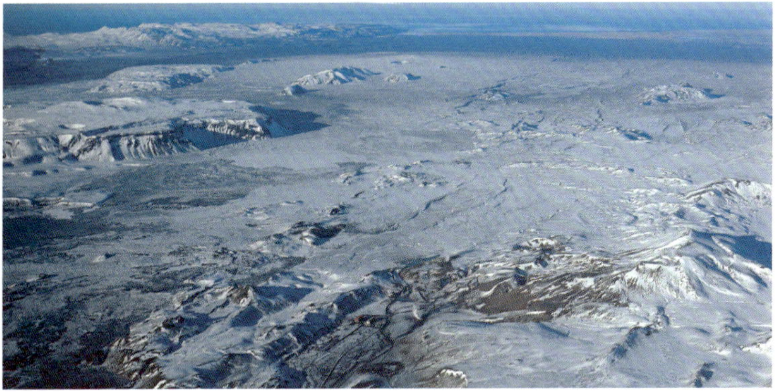

Ásbyrgi is in the *Jökulsárgljúfur* National Park.
Catastrophic floods from *Vatnajökull* with an estimated discharge
of up to 1 million m³/s carved the canyon in prehistoric times.

The National Park of *Jökulsárgljúfur*. *Dettifoss* is the largest waterfall on the *Jökulsá* river and in Europe as well. Looking towards the south. *Dettifoss* in the foreground and *Herðubreið* in the eastern interior highlands in the distance.

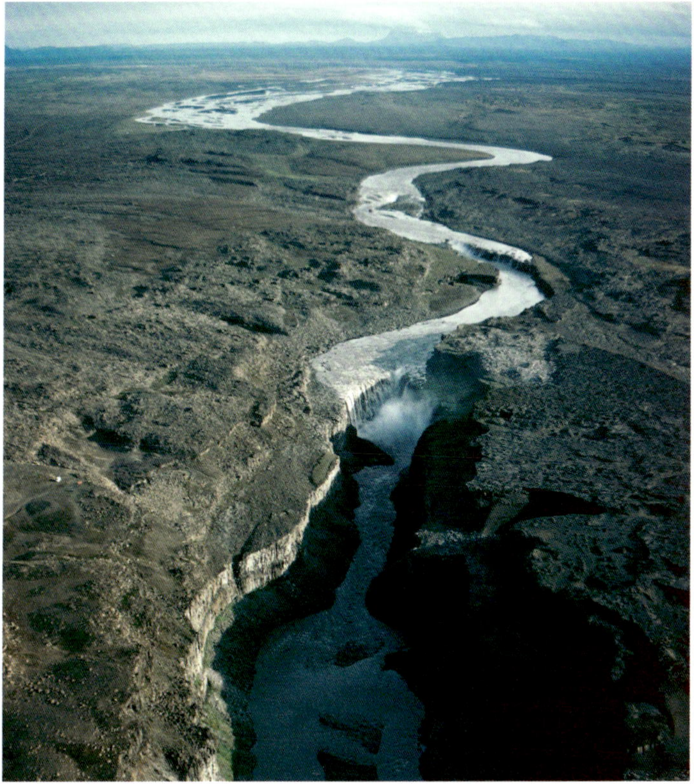

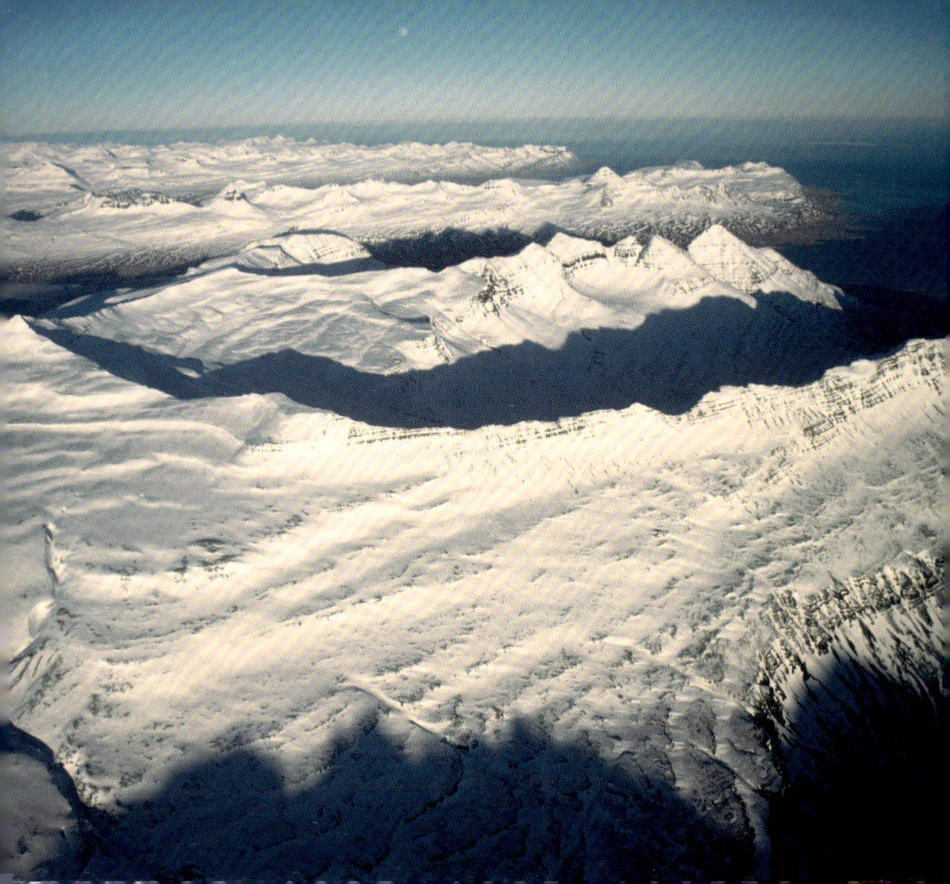

THE EAST

For fifteen million years layer upon layer of lava accumulated. Ice Age glaciers then carved deep troughs into the lava pile, fjords were cut into the coastline and knife edged ridges formed between them. Behind the mountains is the fertile *Hérað* area while beyond lie heaths and snow-capped mountains.

During the Settlement period over 1100 years ago, it is likely that most ships sailed to the Eastern Fjords as this was the closest land when sailing from the west coast of Norway. In many ways the landscape reminded the seamen of their homeland with its high mountains and narrow fjords. More than anything else, these characteristics typify the Eastern Fjords. When flying along these fjords one thinks automatically of the origins of this land mass in the North-Atlantic. Fifteen million years ago the earth's enormous forces combined in a wild ecstasy of creation. Enormous plumes of hot steam rose into the air where magma poured out of huge fissures and into the sea. The forces had already been at work for tens of millions of years building up the foundations of the land from the seafloor.

For fifteen million years the land spread out on both sides from the diverging plate boundary which time and again produced new layers of lava. Volcanic activity has continued with few interruptions up to the present day. Glaciers cut through the land and created fjords with mountain divides between them. A similiar landscape can be found five hundred kilometres away at the other side of the country, in the Western Fjords.

Looking northwards across the Eastern Fjords as far as the eye can see.

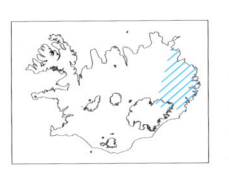

The easternmost valley glacier *Öxarfellsjökull* flows down from the main glacier of *Vatnajökull*. The central volcano *Snæfell*, 1833 m, in the background.

Majestic mountains south of *Dalatangi*
and north of *Mjóifjörður* on the east coast.

Kambanes is a distinctive headland in the central Eastern Fjords. Looking across *Kambanes* towards the settlement of *Stöðvarfjörður* on the fjord of the same name.

Dalatangi at the mouth of *Mjóifjörður* (south of *Seyðisfjörður*).
A meteorological station here has recorded regularly since 1938.

Drift ice from Greenland can always pay a visit but seldom poses any serious threat. In the old days it was known as "The country's ancient enemy".

Skrúður is a precipitous island teeming with birdlife. The island is the remains of a substantial volcanic vent which fed molten lava through the now vanished lava pile during formation of the eastern part of the country 15 million years ago.

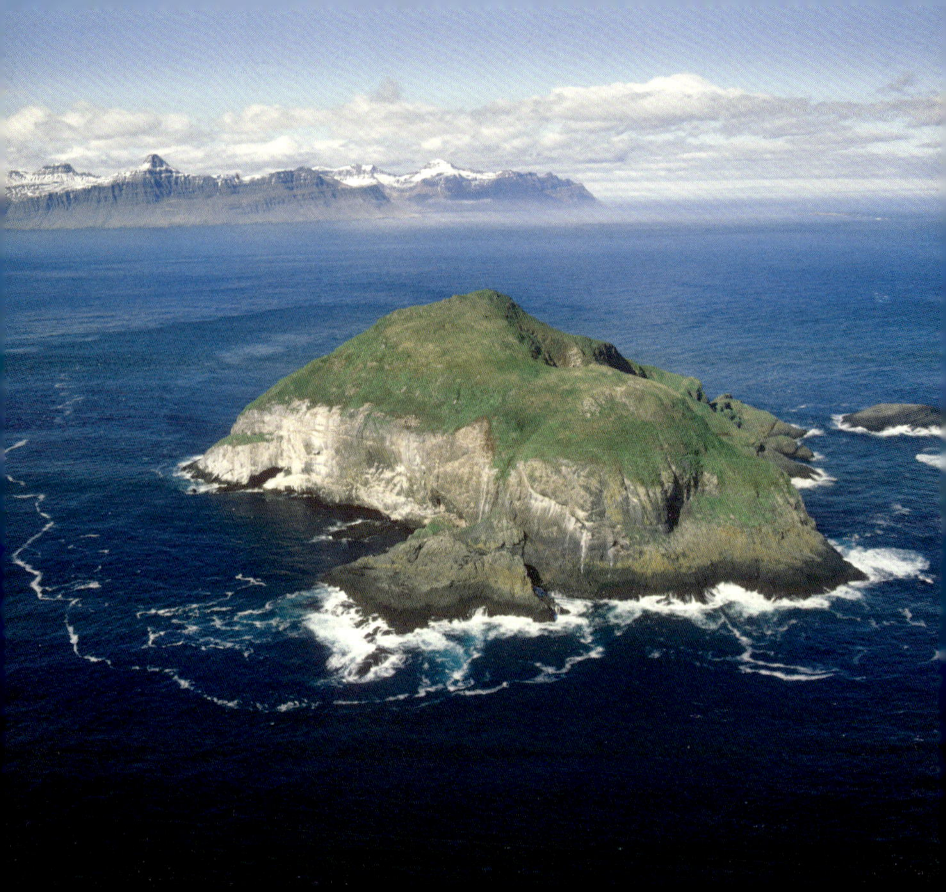

Rauðubjörg is the easternmost point in Iceland. From here to *Bjargtangar* (page 82) farthest west in the country is 517 km measured as the crow flies.

Hengifoss in *Fljótsdalur* cascades through a gorge of colourful ancient strata, which bear witness to true forest vegetation millions of years ago.

Hallormsstaður woodland is one of the few forest areas in Iceland.

115

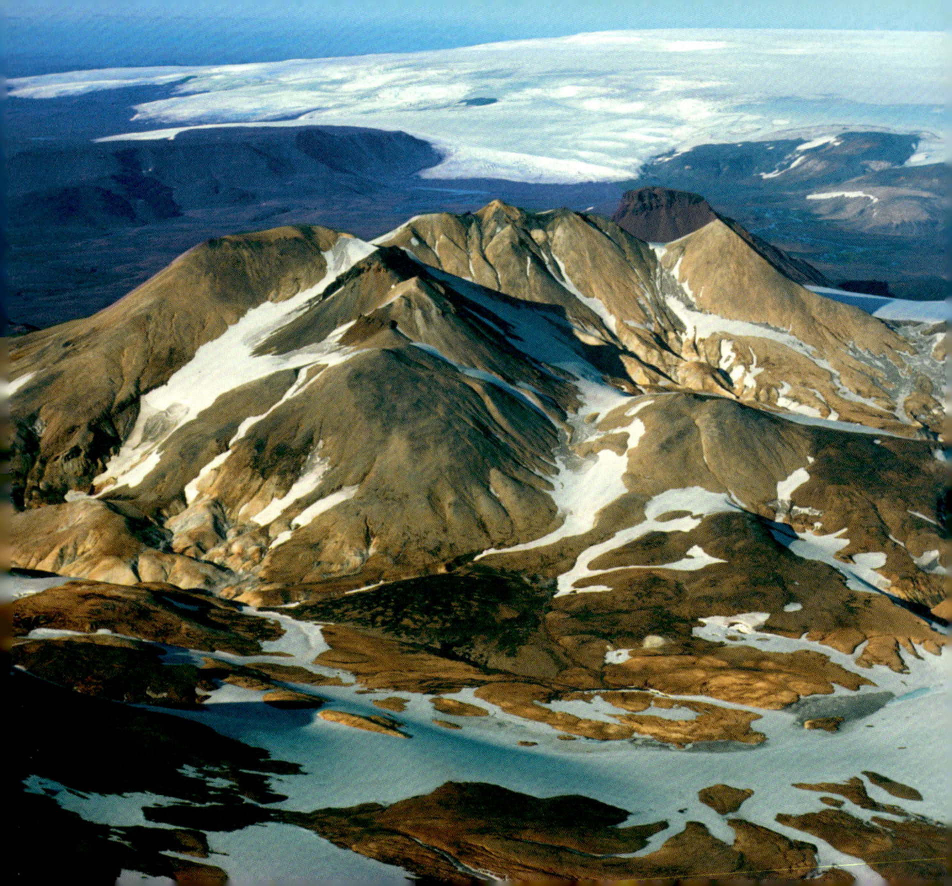

THE INTERIOR HIGHLANDS

The interior region is an area of stark extremes. There are large glaciers, vast areas of moraine-covered terrain, endless horizons of pitch-black lavafields and magnificent volcanoes of diverse origin. Most of the topography is geologically young, and the most outstanding characteristic of this region is its barrenness.

Because of Iceland's location on the Mid-Atlantic Ridge, which causes plate movement in the North-Atlantic, the country is criss-crossed and torn by fractures. This is particularly evident in those areas closest to the active rift zone that runs through the country from southwest to northeast.

Since the Ice Age began about three million years ago glacial periods have alternated with milder interglacial periods. During the glacial periods the majority of the country was covered with glaciers while during the interglacial periods the climate was similar to what it has been over the past ten thousand years. These fluctuations have had a decisive effect on the landscape formation and have dictated the shape and form of the volcanoes.

The landscape of central Iceland is one of incredible contrasts which are especially evident from the air. An immense area north of *Vatnajökull* glacier is covered with dark and sandy lavas that have engulfed the older landscape. There are vast areas of glacial moraine-covered terrain which are almost totally devoid of vegetation. The 8.100 km^2 Vatnajökull is a world of its own, characterised by valleys and rolling hills of ice where white plains of perpetual snow merge with the sky above.

Kerlingarfjöll is a group of rhyolite mountains in the central highlands.

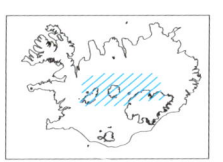

In early 1980 there was a glacial surge in
the south of *Langjökull*. The glacier fractured and surged forward
at 100 metres per day for several weeks. Meltwater abounds in the icefield.

Lake *Löðmundarvatn* in the tranquil autumn atmosphere.

Herðubreið towers majestically above its surroundings. View northwards.

South of *Herðubreið* lies *Askja*, a great caldera 12 km in diameter.
It contains *Öskjuvatn*, the second deepest lake in Iceland, 257 m in depth.

Kverkfjöll in
Vatnajökull, one of the main high temperature geothermal areas in Iceland.

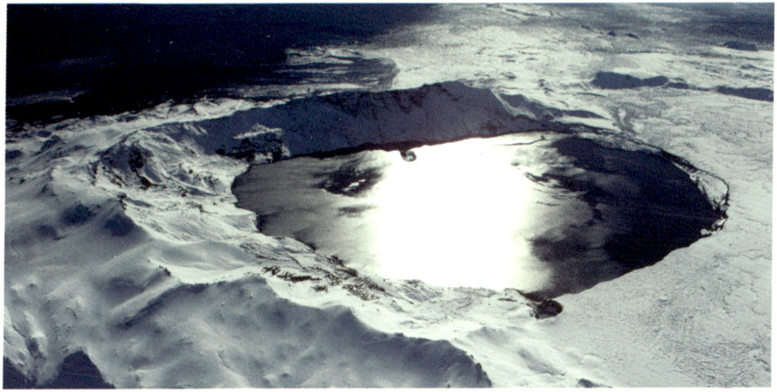

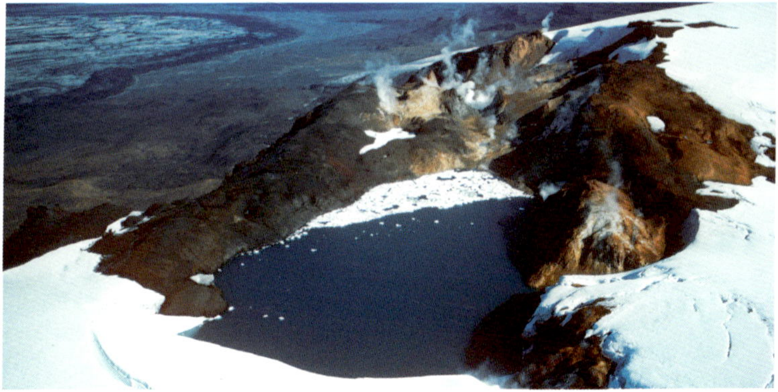

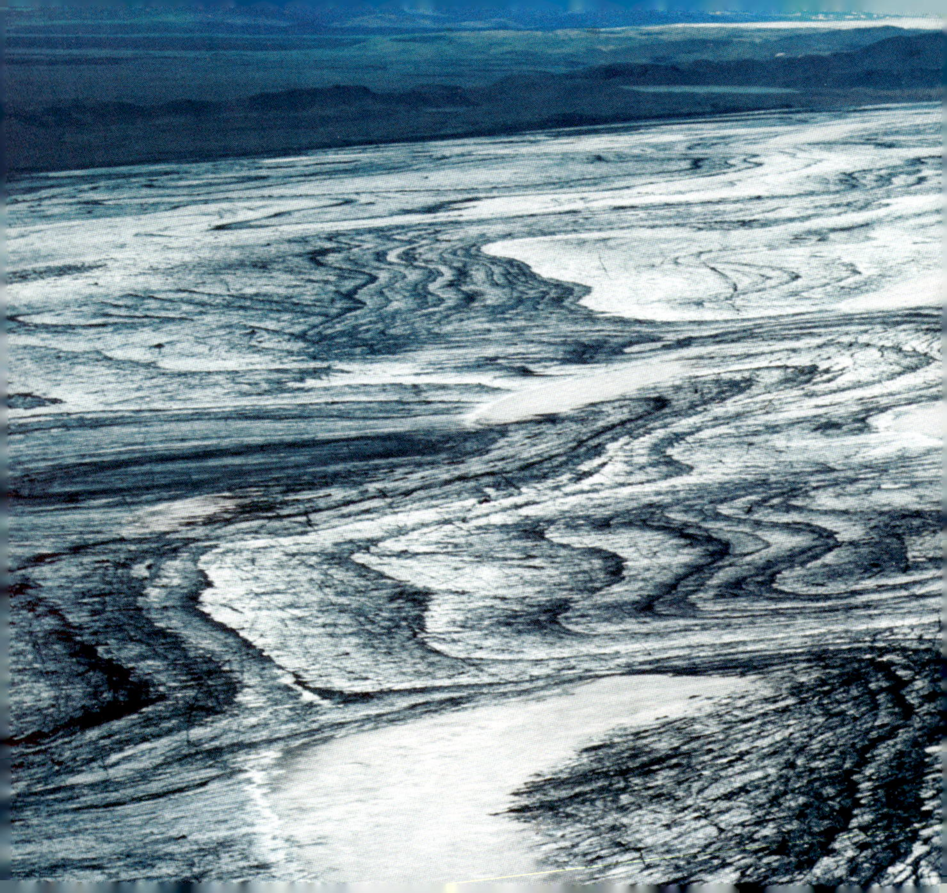

The inland area of *Þórsmörk* bathed in the late evening sun.

TECHNICAL INFORMATION

Most of the photographs in the book are taken with 35mm Nikon and 6x6cm Hasselblad 503CX. Film used was Kodachrome, Ektachrome and Fuji films. Most photographs in the volcanity chapter were taken with Digital Nikon D300 camera. The shutter speed was most often 1/1000 s. Björn Rúriksson flew the photographic trips using low and high-wing single- and multiengine aircraft. He has been flying since 1970. The flight level used was from 500 up to 26.000 feet above the objects.

Hlöðufell is one of
the most beautiful table mountains in the highlands. The mountain
formed in a subglacial eruption during the Ice Age. As the eruption broke
through the ice sheet it became less explosive and the mountain became
capped by a lava shield. *Bláfell* (inland from *Gullfoss*) in centre background.

Skjaldbreiður was formed about 9000 years ago during a continuous lava eruption of long duration from the same crater. Lava flowed incessantly from a central crater and resulted in gentle slopes. Lake *Þingvallavatn* at left background.

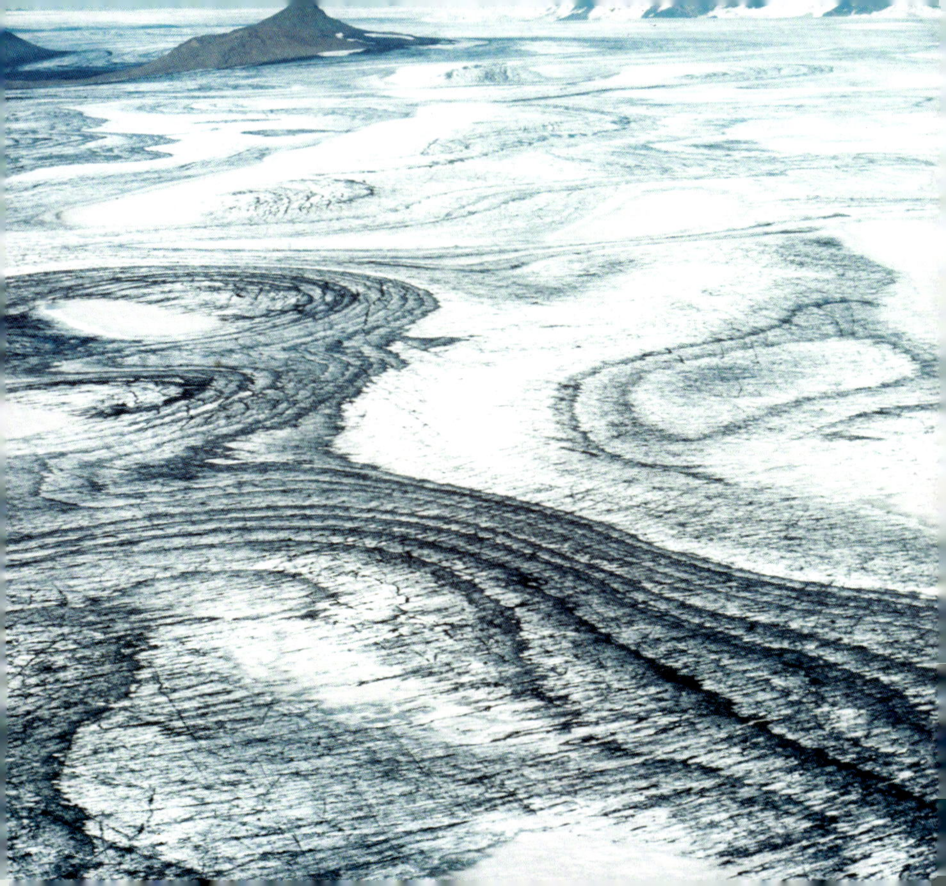

The rhyolite mountain *Pálsfjall* in western *Vatnajökull*.

Lake *Langisjór* is southwest of *Vatnajökull*. The long serrated ridges of rock result from fissure eruptions underneath the ice sheet of the last glacial period.

Pages 122/123: Volcanic ash previously deposited over the snow expanse forms a pattern on the surface of *Tungnaárjökull* in southwestern *Vatnajökull*.